CHANGING LIFE
in Scotland & Britain 1830–1930

Ronald Cameron
(Principal Teacher of History, Tain Royal Academy)

Christine Henderson
(Teacher of History, Kelso High School)

Charles Robertson
(Depute Head Teacher, Earlston High School)

Pulse Publications

CONTENTS

Published and typeset by
Pulse Publications
45 Raith Road, Fenwick,
Ayrshire, KA3 6DB

Printed by
Ritchie of Edinburgh

British Library Cataloguing-in-Publication Data
A Catalogue record for this book is available from the British
Library

ISBN 0 948 766 46 8

© Cameron, Henderson & Robertson 1997

Acknowledgements

The authors and publishers would like to thank the following for permission to reproduce copyright material:

Tain Museum for the loan of the cover photographs; *Punch*
for the use of cartoons on pages 4, 5 and 46; *The Wellcome
Unit for the History of Medicine, Glasgow University* for the
picture on page 6; *The National Museums of Scotland* for
the photographs on page 8 and those in Chapter 3; *The
Illustrated London News* for the prints on pages 9, 10, 11,
13 and 14; *Locheil and the Clan Cameron Museum*,
Achnacarry for the photograph on page 22; *St Andrews
University Library* for the photograph on page 23; *Glasgow Museums* for the photographs on pages 26, 27 and
29; *An Lanntair Gallery*, Stornoway for the loan of prints;
The photographic archive of the *Scottish Mining Museum*
for photographs on pages 52, 53, 58, 60, 61, 62 and the
table on page 64; *The Radio Times Hulton Picture Library*
for illustrations on pages 48, 63 and 88; *Trustees of the
National Library for Scotland* for illustrations on pages 46,
47 and 66; *Blackwell Publications* for documents from
Scottish Economic and Social History by R H Campbell and
JBA Dow and extract from *Railways* by G C Allen; *Imperial
College of Science, Medicine and Technology* for the photograph on page 73; *The National Railway Museum*, York
for LNER poster on page 69; *The Marx Memorial Library*,
London for extracts from the *Memories of Helen Crawfurd;
John Murray Publications* for the People's Charter and
document extracts from *British Industry 1815–1914* by
Peter Lane; *The Museums Education Service*, Glasgow for
photographs on pages 86, 89 and for document extract
from *Scottish Women and the Vote* workpack; Mrs Siobhan
Butterfield for typing Chapters 3, 4 and 5.

Every attempt has been made to contact copyright hold-
ers but we apologise if any have been overlooked.

POPULATION CHANGE IN SCOTLAND

What you will learn:

- ☞ that the population of Britain increased for many reasons
- ☞ that the factors controlling population growth changed constantly during the period
- ☞ that dramatic changes took place in the distribution of Scotland's population
- ☞ that some people left the Highlands of their own free will
- ☞ that many more people were forced to leave
- ☞ that evictions were halted only because of a violent up-rising of the poorest people

▬ CONCEPTS ▬

Birth rate
Death rate
Natural increase
Eviction
Social change
Economic change
Mono-culture
Environmental degredation

Population Change (Scotland and Britain)

Year	Population Eng. & Wales	Population Scotland	% Increase Scotland	Birth Rate[1]	Death Rate[1]	Ratio of F to M[2]
1755	6,500,000	1,265,380	N/A	N/A	N/A	N/A
1801	8,900,000	1,608,420	N/A	N/A	N/A	117.6
1811	10,164,000	1,805,864	12.3	N/A	N/A	118.5
1821	12,000,000	2,091,521	15.8	N/A	N/A	112.9
1831	13,897,000	2,364,386	13.0	N/A	N/A	112.2
*1841	15,928,000	2,620,184	10.8	30.3	22.4	111.0
1851	17,972,000	2,888,742	10.2	N/A	N/A	110.0
1861	20,066,000	3,062,294	6.0	35.1	22.1	111.2
1871	22,712,000	3,360,018	9.7	35.0	22.7	109.6
1881	25,974,000	3,735,573	11.2	33.3	19.6	107.6
1891	29,003,000	4,025,647	7.8	30.5	19.0	107.2
1901	32,528,000	4,472,103	11.1	29.2	17.1	105.7
1911	36,070,000	4,760,904	6.5	25.4	15.7	106.2
1921	37,887,000	4,882,497	2.6	23.0	13.9	108.0
1931	39,952,000	4,842,980	-0.8	18.2	13.2	108.4
1951	43,758,000	5,095,969	5.2	17.9	12.4	109.3

[1] Birth Rate & Death Rate figures expressed per thousand.
[2] Ratio of Females to 100 Males.
* Figures for England and Wales—Scottish figures not available until 1856.

Table 1.1 **Sources:** *Scottish Population Statistics* by James Gray Kyd. *Standard Grade History* by Rigg, Teale and Mackay. *British Economic and Social History* by P. Sauvain

THE WAY in which a country's population changes over time can reveal many fascinating things about both the health of its people and its economy. The first reasonably reliable attempt at a census, or population count, in Scotland was made in 1755 by the Rev. Alexander Webster who calculated that Scotland at that time contained 1,265,380 people. The government held the first official British census in 1801 and has repeated the exercise every ten years since then. Since 1836 in England and Wales and 1855 in Scotland, all births, deaths and marriages have had to be officially registered. This development has enabled us to work out birth and death rates and, along with other records, to piece together a general picture of what was happening to Scotland's population. (See Table 1.1)

The simple statistics of growth conceal a complex pattern of change and movement. Although the population showed a 'natural increase', since births exceeded deaths, the story is complicated by emigration, immigration and migration within Scotland itself.

At the start of our period (1830) the population was increasing rapidly. In 1989 Scotland had a birth rate of 12.5 per thousand and a death rate of 12 per thousand. This means that for every thousand people living in the country 12 died and 12.5 were born. Scottish figures are unknown, but back in 1836 the birth rate in England and Wales was 30.3 per thousand while, to counterbalance this a little, 22.4 per thousand 'popped their clogs'. It does not need a mathematical genius to calculate that the 'natural increase' was about 8 per thousand. By 1871, in Scotland the birth rate was 35 per thousand, while the angel of death had made off with 22.6 per thousand. The natural increase had soared to 12.4 per thousand. What could be the reasons behind all this frenetic activity—this hatching and dispatching? A number of factors seem to have been at work.

Child Labour

The 18th century saw rapid industrialisation in Britain. Hideous, smoky factory towns grew up in what had been a predominantly rural environment. These towns offered jobs to men, women and children. The hours were long, the pay was bad and the conditions of work were utterly appalling. However, people sensed that survival was made easier by having lots of children whom they could take to work with them in mines and factories. People got married early and had enormous families. The eighth child might be called Octavius or Octavia since, by that stage, many parents had run out of names and resorted to a type of numbering. Often more than one child was called after a parent as it was assumed that several would die young.

Early Marriages

Early marriages also were also common in rural areas. In the Highlands, in 1800, illegal whisky distilling and smuggling was an enormously successful industry. There were 200 illegal stills in Glenlivet alone and an incalculable number in Argyll. Since Highland whisky was better and cheaper than the produce of licensed Lowland stills, business was brisk. However, whisky making was a team game. Every smuggler needed a wife to create the uisge beatha (water of life) while he was away selling her wares in Glasgow or Edinburgh. This led to early marriage and lots of little distillers. Sadly, in 1821 the government took steps to crush this thriving enterprise and transfer produc-

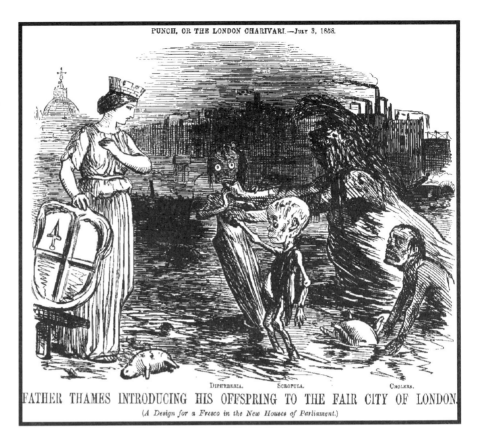

PUNCH, OR THE LONDON CHARIVARI.—July 3, 1858.

DIPHTHERIA. SCROFULA. CHOLERA.

FATHER THAMES INTRODUCING HIS OFFSPRING TO THE FAIR CITY OF LONDON.
(A Design for a Fresco in the New Houses of Parliament.)

tion to official whisky factories. Large families were also useful in the Western Isles in the kelp industry which flourished between about 1760 and 1820. Families worked knee-deep in the sea to harvest seaweed which was dried and burned in order to make soda ash for soap and glass manufacture.

Improvements to Food Supply

All these extra mouths required a great deal of extra food. The population could not have grown as it did if there had not been huge changes in farming methods in the mid to late 1700s. These changes are called the agricultural revolution and they resulted in big increases in food production. Numbers of any species will increase if its food supply increases. For example, during the First World War (1914 to 1918) lots of soldiers were killed and left unburied because their bodies were in very dangerous places. Rats ate the bodies. There were lots of bodies and soon the battlefields were infested with huge numbers of rats. People have more in

common with rats than we like to admit.

The improved food supply in the 1700s probably helped to hold down the death rate since more food made people stronger and more able to survive illnesses and disease.

Falling Birth Rate

The fall in the birth rate after 1871 can be readily understood. With the collapse of the kelp industry and whisky smuggling, early marriage was expensive and less attractive to Highland folk. In 1842 women and children under 10 were forbidden to work with their menfolk underground in coal mines. The government passed several laws which gradually excluded child labour from textile mills and other factories. In 1870 in England and 1872 in Scotland parents were required by law to send their little ones to school.

Children became immensely unprofitable and a financial burden. They came to be much less fashionable and many people

4

began to have fewer. The growing middle class went for quality rather than quantity in the knowledge that fewer children would leave them with more money for other things. They were helped in this quest by technological changes in rubber production which enabled satisfactory condoms to be manufactured towards the end of the 19th century.

The birth rate plummeted from 35 per thousand in 1871 to 18.2 per thousand in 1931. The birth rate also fell because there was a shortage of men in Britain. More men than women emigrated and 750,000 of them were killed in the First World War. By 1930 there were 2 million 'surplus' women in Britain, most of whom remained childless. This can be seen from the 'Ratio of Females to Males' column in Table 1.1 on page 3. Despite the fall in the birth rate the population continued to increase because the death rate fell too. There are a number of reasons for this.

Improved Public Health
Throughout history, Scotland's population has been regularly culled by dreadful epidemics. In the Middle Ages there was the 'Black Death', in the 17th century the plague and in the 19th century cholera.

People had some very dirty habits and they paid the price. There was no rubbish collection system, so rats thrived and rats spread disease. By 1770 the City Fathers of Glasgow and Edinburgh had just about succeeded in persuading their people not to throw their own excrement out of the windows. This was a big improvement, but unfortunately there were no proper sewers so sewage often found its way into burns and rivers which supplied drinking water. Be warned! Drinking water contaminated

with sewage is a very unhealthy habit! It led to a new disease, cholera, which came from India and carried away huge numbers of the population in major epidemics between 1831 and 1867. Public Health Acts in 1848 and 1897 empowered councils to provide clean water and attend to sewage disposal. The death rate fell—even if the water seemed a little tasteless!

Better Housing
During the 19th century the population of British cities often grew very quickly. Liverpool's population went from 138,000 to 286,000 between 1821 and 1841— more than doubling in 20 years. (See *Punch* cartoon of 1852 'A Court for King Cholera'.) Housing was a massive problem for the poor who flocked to these cities. Private landlords rented space in damp, dirty, cold, badly ventilated slums. Until 1851 there was a tax on windows, with a resulting lack of fresh air. Killer diseases like scarlet fever, diphtheria, tuberculosis and scrofula are spread by infected droplets of water in the air. In the Victo-

rian slums the poor breathed in each other's germs and died in droves. Towards the end of the century the government gave the power to local councils to clear the worst slums and later to build good, cheap houses for rent. Increasing prosperity also improved the housing stock. Better houses led to fewer deaths.

Better medicine
Medical knowledge and practice made significant progress during the 19th century. In the 18th century smallpox had been a great killer and many survivors' pockmarked faces bore testimony to the ravages of this dreadful disease. The principle of vaccinating people against it was discovered as early as 1796 by Edward Jenner, a Scottish trained doctor working in England. Jenner knew that country folk believed that those who caught cowpox, a milder disease which milkmaids were likely to catch, were safe from smallpox. He took fluid from the sores of a cowpox sufferer and rubbed it into cuts on uninfected people.

A COURT FOR KING CHOLERA.

They did not catch smallpox. Although the practice of vaccination was strongly opposed on religious and moral grounds, deaths from smallpox fell from about 3,000 per million in 1800 to 500 per million in 1840.

In 1853 the government introduced a compulsory vaccination programme for all babies. Despite strenuous opposition from those who saw this an attack on individual freedom, the scheme helped to reduce the death rate considerably in the last quarter of the 19th century.

At the start of the 19th century hospitals were shunned because they were seen as places where people died—usually from a disease they did not have when they entered! If a surgical operation was necessary and possible, wealthy people would prefer to have it done at home on the dining room table. There were no anaesthetics, so patients had to face the surgeon's knife and saw fully conscious. The survival rate for the amputation of major limbs was not encouraging, especially since the instruments were not sterilised. A quick wipe with a damp cloth before the first cut was considered to be enough, so many died from postoperative infections and shock. This unfortunate state of affairs was turned around by three developments.

Clean Hospitals
Florence Nightingale (1820–1910) came to prominence when she was nursing British soldiers wounded in southern Russia during the Crimean War (1854–56). When she arrived at the British military hospital in Scutari, Turkey, many of the wounded were dying of cholera. She insisted on the novel idea that hospitals should be clean. She demanded that army engineers build sewers and lay on clean

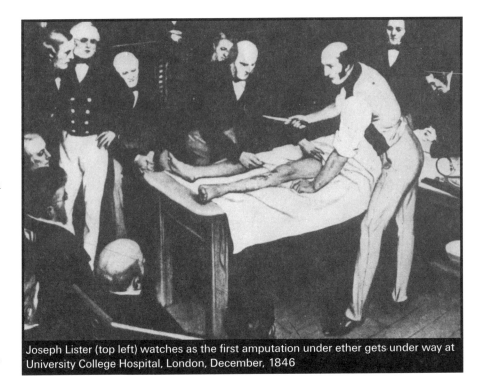

Joseph Lister (top left) watches as the first amputation under ether gets under way at University College Hospital, London, December, 1846

water supplies. She, and her team of volunteer nurses, washed sheets and blankets and fed the patients on wholesome food. Many said, "the silly woman is wasting her time", but death rates fell and Nightingale's ideas became standard nursing practice in British hospitals.

Safe Anaesthetics
After decades of experimentation within the medical profession, James Y Simpson (1811–70) perfected the use of chloroform as the first reasonable safe and effective anaesthetic for childbirth and surgery. You could now have your leg cut off without having to watch! He was much criticised at the time by those who thought that pain was something to be endured, but his ideas gained widespread acceptance after Queen Victoria used chloroform during the birth of her son, Leopold, in 1853. Of course people continued to develop infections and die after surgery.

Effective Antiseptics
Joseph Lister (1827–1912), Professor of Surgery at Glasgow University, studied the work of the

French scientist, Louis Pasteur, on germs and infection. This led him to use carbolic to sterilise dressings, surgical instruments, the surgeon's hands and the patients' wounds. Survival rates in Lister's operations improved from 55% in 1864 to 85% in 1869.

These developments must have been a factor in the falling death rate. Medicine continued to improve dramatically in the early part of the 20th century. During the First World War many wounded soldiers died from loss of blood. The introduction of blood transfusions by the American Army cut these losses significantly. The adoption of the technique by civilian hospitals after the war made further inroads into the death rate.

Less Alcoholism
There is an old Scottish saying that water is a fine drink if taken in the right spirit. During the 19th century however, Scottish people continued to drink less and less whisky and more and more tea, a trend which had begun in the previous century. Whisky can do wicked things to the liver, tea does not.

FUADACH NAN GAIDHEIL: THE HIGHLAND CLEARANCES

The effects of agricultural and industrial change on the different regions of Scotland are summarised in Table 1.2. You will notice that the population of the Highland, or Northern, area continued to increase until 1861 and then began to fall. Of course there were local variations. In Argyll the population peaked in 1831, in Inverness it was in 1841, and Sutherland and Ross-shire's maximum was in 1851. The case study of Gruinards (page 9) will give you a clue to one of the reasons why the Highland population first of all increased more slowly than that of the Lowlands and then fell. The reason is that people were evicted from their homes. There were, unfortunately, many reasons why people were forced to leave their homes.

THE HIGHLAND CLEARANCES: 1760 TO 1830

In order to understand properly the situation during our period (1830 to 1930), we need to look briefly at the events of the years beforehand.

Change in Highland Society

After the disastrous Jacobite rebellion of 1745–46, Highland clan chiefs ceased to regard the clanspeople as their own kin. In the old days a large population gave them a good following of fiercely loyal fighting men. That all came to an end on Culloden moor. The chiefs began to spend most of their time in Edinburgh or London and looked to their lands to supply them with a lot of money in rent in order to provide them with the luxurious lifestyle of the great lords of southern Britain. Oatmeal and loyalty would no longer be enough. Initially they began to demand higher and higher rents

which were to be paid in cash rather than in produce or labour service, as had been the old way. Thus, in 1845, when the people of Glen Calvie in Easter Ross were evicted, they were paying £55 a year in rent for land which a *Times* reporter thought might fetch £15 in England. Many tacksmen, or sub-chiefs, refused to pay these higher rents and led their people into exile in America. They were unwilling to pay Lothian levels of rent for poor Highland land.

The Sheep Factor

Towards the end of the 18th century the price of wool increased dramatically. From about 1760, people in various Highland communities received legal notices to quit land which their families had occupied since time immemorial. This was to make way for 'Na coaraich mora', the great sheep, brought in by southern farmers who were willing, at least in the short term, to pay the high rents.

Traditionally, Highland people did not keep a lot of sheep, usually only a few of their own small animals which they called by name, took into their homes at night and plucked when they

wanted wool. They were not thought to have the skills needed to farm the big Lowland sheep and were not given the opportunity to acquire them. Evictions for sheep farming continued without let up until after 1850. The most notorious were the Sutherland Clearances between 1800 and 1815. Patrick Sellar and James Loch, servants of the Countess of Sutherland, drove most of the people from the landward areas of the county, burning the homes of many. Similar events happened throughout the Highlands and Islands, affecting almost every parish. This poses the question 'If clearance was so widespread why did the population continue to rise and not fall sooner?'

The Need for Cheap Labour

Highland people had been emigrating to the Americas since the 1600s. There is a tale of people from Lochaber arriving in North Carolina to be met at the ship by a black slave who greeted them in good North Argyll Gaelic. One woman turned to her man and said "A Dhia nan Gras, am bith sinn cho dubh ris a bhalach seo fhein?" (Oh God of Grace, will we be as black as this boy himself?) Most of those evicted saw

Population of Scottish Regions

District	Population (thousands)	Percentage of Total	Density (People per sq. mile)
1755			
Northern	652	51	31
Central	464	37	110
Southern	149	11	36
1861			
Northern	1020	33	48
Central	1769	58	414
Southern	273	9	65
1951			
Northern	1000	20	47
Central	3840	75	900
Southern	256	5	61

Table 1.2

Source: Adapted from *Scottish Population Statistics* by James Gray Kyd. (The Central Belt consists of the Counties of Ayr, Dumbarton, Lanark, Renfrew, Clackmannan, Stirling, the Lothians, Fife and the City of Dundee.)

Evicted Highland family in the ruins of their home

Canada or America as the place to go. This did not suit the landowners who wanted to keep the people as cheap labour while turning their land into sheep farms.

The trend was set during the Sutherland clearances when many who had lost their homes were settled on tiny patches of uncultivated ground, later to be known as crofts, along the coast. Sellar, writing in 1815, made his intentions clear "...the interior should be possessed by Cheviot shepherds and the people brought down to the coast and placed there in lotts under the size of three acres, sufficient for the maintenance of an industrious family, but pinched enough to cause them to turn their attention to fishing..." (quoted by James Hunter in *The Making of the Crofting Community.*) Others would find work in the woollen mills to be established at nearby Brora. If sufficient money could be made by fishing, the crofters could pay high rents for their patches of ground. Although they were terrified of the sea a few brave souls did try to fish, but some were drowned and the scheme was never a big success. Safe harbours are few and far between on the north coast of

Scotland and boats which were suitable for those fierce seas were not available.

Fishing was, however, an important source of income for many island people. Many of the men got seasonal work as crew on the large boats from east coast ports, while women and girls worked as gutters and packers. The herring girls, 'clann nighean an sgadain', migrated from fishing port to fishing port—Stornoway, Lerwick, Wick, Peterhead, Aberdeen, Great Yarmouth, Lowestoft—following the herring fleet and the shoals of herring. This provided them with an additional cash income which helped to pay the rent on their crofts. Supported by fishing, the population of Lewis continued to increase until 1901, long after the population of the rest of the Highlands had gone into decline. In the Western Isles, landowners were making huge sums from the kelp industry. Again evicted people were given little crofts and the chance to earn a little money if the whole family worked at the kelp. In north Argyll men got work in the slate quarries of Ballachulish, Easdale and the island of Belnahua. In Strontian there were leadmines which were working before 1745.

In the first years of the 19th century there was much alarm at the reluctancc of Highlanders to stay and a fear that the whole area would be depopulated, making it difficult for the army to get recruits and denying the lairds cheap labour. The landowners therefore had little trouble persuading the government to pass the Passenger Vessels Act of 1803. This laid down safety standards for emigrant ships, limited the number of passengers they could carry and regulated the amounts of food, water and medicine they were to carry. As a result the cost of emigrating rose from £3 10s (£3.50p) to over £10. The tide of emigration was stemmed.

Ethnic Cleansing
Some of the people who carried out the clearances had deep racial prejudices against Highland people. Patrick Sellar called them "barbaroush hordes" and said their language, Gaelic, was an obstacle to all progress and had to be eradicated. He sought to replace the Gaels with English speakers whom he considered to be superior.

Overpopulation?
Many apologists for the clearances suggest that the Highlands were overpopulated and that the landowners were doing the peasant population a favour by evicting them and sending them on their way to the good life in Greenock or Geelong. This idea was first popular with the landownwers themselves, but later would be rejected by historians like Ian Grimble, John Prebble and James Hunter who could point out that the Highlands actually has a greater population today but is now regarded as being sparsely populated. Clearance and eviction left huge tracts of land empty while creating seriously

The Highland Clearances
Gruinards
Strath Carron, South Sutherland
March 1854

Highland Women

THEY WERE on the road long before the court officer and the police arrived at dawn. It isn't clear how the violence began. The women were accused of having pelted the police with stones and mud. Others claim that the police 'had a dram on them' and that the order to clear the road was given in English only, a language which few of the Ross women understood, and then the police charged.

The size of the crowd is also the subject of dispute. The police say there were 300 men and women. Donald Ross, solicitor and journalist, said that there were only 60 women and children. The injuries are not in dispute. No policemen were hurt. A number of batons were broken and many women suffered severe cuts to the backs of their heads. There were a number of fractured skulls and some died of their injuries or suffered brain damage.

In defending the action of the police, Sheriff MacKenzie made it clear that these people were persistent troublemakers. He claimed that they had stripped naked a sheriff's officer with an order for their eviction and giggling, carried him to the parish boundaries. Donald Ross said they did not hurt or embarrass him in any way. Sheriff Mackenzie said that this history of lawlessness goes back to 1792, Bliadhna nan caoraich, the year of the sheep, when the men of the Glen tried to drive all the sheep out of Sutherland. They were well on their way to Inverness when the arrival of the army caused them to abandon 6,000 sheep near Alness.

The women said this happened 60 years ago, before they were born. What is clear is that after the events of 31 March 1854, sheep could safely graze on land which the Ross women of Gruinards had long regarded as theirs and had defended with tenacity. This was their last stand. In history there are no second prizes and the winner takes all.

9

congested crofting townships. This overcrowding was then seen as being a cause for further evictions.

Modern development economists accept that a dense population can have benefits. In the 1930s British colonial agricultural officials had given up on the Kenyan district of Machakos. They blamed its overpopulation for severe soil erosion. Today Machakos is neatly terraced. Useful trees grow on terrace margins with the soil erosion under control. The houses are much better than they were 60 years ago but the population has increased fivefold. The high population density has forced the Wakamba, (the people who live there), to adopt better methods of cultivation. However, there are enough people around to provide a wide range of services and employment in manufacturing. The Highlands were denied the opportunity to meet the challenge.

The Situation in 1830
Despite seventy years of eviction, the population was still rising, mainly because of the availability of part-time work in many areas. Eviction had, however, concentrated the population in dangerously congested crofting communities which would be very vulnerable should anything go wrong with their sources of food and income. In the period 1820 to 1860 these communities were beset by a series of disasters which encouraged the landowners to carry out further evictions.

REASONS FOR THE HIGHLAND CLEARANCES 1830 TO 1886

Failure of Kelp and Whisky
In 1825 the government removed the tax on imported soda ash and by 1827 the kelp industry had ceased to be profitable. Landowners no longer looked on the crofters as a useful seasonal work force. Since the government had crushed the whisky trade in 1821, many found it hard to find money to pay their outrageous rents. Eviction seemed to be the answer. In 1827 the Passenger Vessels Act of 1803 was done away with to encourage emigration again. Most Highlanders were too poor to emigrate and their chiefs too poor to pay to get rid of them. Despite this, MacLean of Coll paid for 300 people to leave Rum

Searching for potatoes in a stubble field, c 1849. *Illustrated London News*

and Lord MacDonald helped 1,300 to leave Uist between 1838 and 1843. The failure of the kelp industry caused Orkney landowners to seek better rents by joining smallholdings to create bigger arable farms. Again, there were evictions.

The Potato Famine

Crowded together in congested townships, with tiny holdings of land, crofters were heavily dependent on potatoes for survival. No other crop could yield so much food from so little Highland soil. At first they were not always popular. Clanranald, a MacDonald chief, introduced them to South Uist in 1743. "You can make us plant these worthless things," the people said, "but, Virgin Mary, you won't make us eat them!" They were wrong. Dependency and addiction soon followed. In 1846 a cruel thing happened. Blight, a potato disease, virtually wiped out the crop. A similar problem affected Ireland, where a million

people died of starvation. In the Highlands desperate people hunted the beaches for shellfish. Weakened by hunger, many died of disease. The only two deaths which the authorities would admit were caused by starvation occurred on Barra. The problem dragged on until 1856. The government appointed Sir Edward Pine Coffin to head a famine relief scheme. Sir Edward was basically a decent and generous man, but his political masters insisted on extracting a high price from those who got help. Men and women were expected to labour all day building 'destitution' roads, dykes and ditches for a starvation ration of oatmeal.

The most effective help provided at this time came from voluntary donations from people in Lowland Scotland (who were often poor themselves), the Free Church of Scotland and from Scottish people living in America. A very few landowners,

notably Lord Lovat in Morar, MacLeod of Dunvegan, MacLean of Argour and Sir James Matheson in Lewis ran commendable relief schemes for their tenants, but to most landowners the famine was regarded as proof that the land was overcrowded and the solution was to arrange for the people to emigrate immediately.

The years 1848 to 1855 were years of mass eviction in the islands where the sheep economy had yet to be established. The mainland was less affected since most of the better land was already under sheep.

Changes in the Poor Law

Under the old Scots Poor Law, landowners were meant to contribute to the poor relief fund for their parish. Highland landowners had traditionally ignored this obligation. In 1846 the government made it clear that the Scots Poor Law was to be applied in

The Prince of Wales shooting deer in the Highlands. *Illustrated London News* 1883 "While big guns play games with the land of my birth." Runrig, *Tear Down These Walls*

the Highlands. This encouraged landowners to evict the poor rather than pay for their occasional relief.

The Bankruptcy of Highland Lairds

The failure of the kelp industry finally pushed many landowners in the islands and North West over the brink into bankruptcy. Serious debts had been a long-running problem with Highland lairds generally, since they tried to rival the luxurious lifestyle of rich Lowland lairds. Many of them were forced to sell all or part of their lands. A number of the estates were bought by successful business tycoons from the south who had money to invest in them. They were keen to get rid of the 'surplus population' and were able to pay for them to emigrate to Canada, America or, by that stage, Australia.

Eviction to Create Deer Forests

Australian wool began to arrive in Scotland about 1820. By 1880 this had rendered sheep farming much less profitable. Sheep farmers also found that the land could carry far fewer sheep than they had at first thought. Heavy grazing with sheep greatly reduced the fertility of land over the years and yields fell, as did the rents sheep farmers were willing to pay. Angus MacKay, aged 22, told a government investigation that crofters in his part of Sutherland were paying 1s 3d (6.5p) per acre for poor land while sheep farmers paid only 8d (3.5p) rent per acre for much better land. The falling profitability of sheep farming forced landowners to turn to other means of getting money. The building of railways in the Highands made holiday travel much easier. Rich business people and aristocrats in the South were willing to pay huge

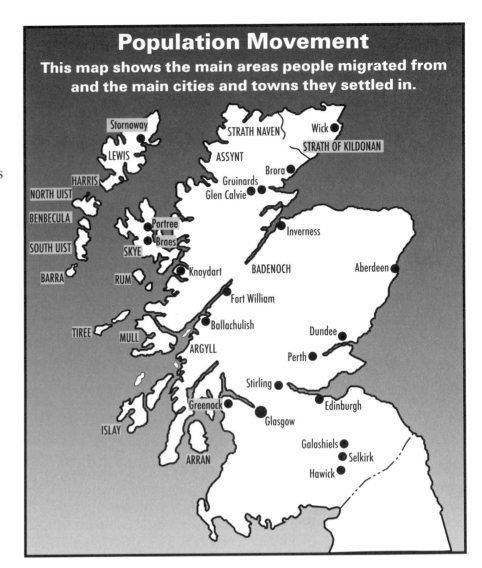

Population Movement

This map shows the main areas people migrated from and the main cities and towns they settled in.

amounts to rent shooting estates in the North where they could go in the autumn to hunt deer and grouse. Some sheep farms were converted to deer estates and some more natives were evicted.

Emigration from the Highlands

As we have noted, the population of all Highland counties began to fall between 1831 and 1861, a trend which was not reversed until the 1960s. This was mainly caused by clearance and emigration. After 1830 emigration began to increase sharply. In 1844 Sir James Matheson bought the Island of Lewis, having made a fortune trading in the Far East, especially in the opium trade with China. He paid for 2,230 people to go to Canada and sent them with enough cash to make a new life there. The

same cannot be said of John Gordon of Cluny who evicted 3,000 people from South Uist, Barra and Benbecula between 1848 and 1851 and added their holdings to his sheep farms. Those who tried to resist were rounded up by men with dogs, bound hand and foot and thrown onto the boats. Those who did not die of disease on the overcrowded ships were set loose in Canada with only a few rags to keep them warm in the hard Canadian winter, no hope of work and scarcely enough English to beg for bread. After 1850 the Highlands and Islands Emigration Commission used funds from landlords, the government and from famine relief charities to finance emigration to Canada and Australia.

After the First World War the

government of Canada ran an assisted passage scheme for Scots, who were guaranteed a job on arrival. Thousands went from all over Scotland. Huge passenger ships were chartered to carry the emigrants. The departure of the *Marloch* and *Metagama* from Stornoway in the early 1920s is still deeply etched in the folk memories of the outer islands.

Migration Within Scotland

Table 1.2 on page 7 shows the constant growth of the population of central Scotland. This is due in part to a north–south drift of population as Highland people were attracted to jobs in the growing industries of the central belt or else were forced to move there by eviction. Working conditions in the mines and factories of central Scotland were so bad that only the desperate would take them. The local population of Lanark, Glasgow and other central belt towns would only take these jobs as a very last resort. Thus employers were often desperate for labour. In 1772 Alexander MacDonnel, a priest in the Braes of Badenoch (Kingussie, Newtonmore, Aviemore) found jobs for 800 of his people with Glasgow factory owners who promised to protect them. Highlanders were usually disliked in the south since many, at that time, were Catholics and few spoke anything but Gaelic. Irish migrants were, at first, more desperate, more numerous and willing to work for even less money.

The invention of steamships and the building of railways made migration, both seasonal and permanent, easier. As the Clyde's heavy engineering industry mushroomed after 1850, more and more Highlanders moved south. By 1900 the Glasgow police force contained huge numbers of men from the Highlands and Islands while many of the women became either nurses in hospitals or domestic servants.

Urbanisation

Events like the Highland clearances rarely happened in other European countries like Denmark, Norway or Switzerland because the peasants there had rights in law and could not be evicted. Clearances happened throughout Britain—those in the Highlands were merely the last. After 1881 the population of the border counties began to decline. They too had undergone a process of agricultural improvement whereby many tenant farmers and their holdings joined together to form one large farm. The introduction of modern methods of farming and mechanisation meant that fewer workers were needed.

The 1870s and 1880s were decades of poor prices for farm produce, so farmers could afford fewer workers. The displaced people were forced to look for work in the growing mill towns of Hawick, Galashiels and Selkirk, or beyond in central Scotland or even Canada, the USA, Australia or New Zealand.

While the population of England and Wales in 1951 was five times that of 1801, the population of

Aignish, Lewis 1888. Crofters confront police and marines two years after the Crofting Act. Aignish was returned to crofting. ILN.

Police and soldiers arrest rioting crofters on the Isle of Lewis. *Illustrated London News,* 1888.

Scotland had only trebled, leading one historian, James G Kyd, to claim that Scotland has lost more people to emigration than any other country in Europe.

CROFTING

The Crofters Act 1886
In 1886 a special law was passed which gave Highland crofters the sort of rights enjoyed by peasants in mainland western Europe. Among many other provisions it

- made it impossible for them to be evicted if they paid their rent. This is called 'security of tenure'.

- allowed the croft to be passed on to the next generation when the crofter died or retired.

- set up a special organisation, the Crofters Commission, to supervise crofting affairs.

- established a Land Court to set fair rents and settle disputes between crofters or between crofters and their landlords.

Why, you might ask, did the Parliament of Great Britain decide to place Highland crofters in a position of security not enjoyed by other British tenant farmers? The reason was the Crofters War.

The Crofters War
Crofters became slightly more prosperous between 1855 and 1880. Evictions became less common and they became more confident. They had finally lost all notion of clanship or kinship with the landowner. Radical journalists, like John Murdoch, editor of *The Highlander,* reminded them of the old Gaelic idea that land belonged to the people as a whole and was not something to be bought and sold. Many island men worked as deck hands on fishing boats

working off Ireland and out of Irish ports. Since they spoke broadly the same language as the Irish, they learned of the Irish land struggle. Irish peasants, faced with a similar but worse situation to their own, had joined the Land League formed by Michael Davitt. They refused to pay rent and some burned the crops and the houses belonging to the English-speaking, Protestant land-owners. This was all quite routine in Irish politics. Their demands were presented in Parliament by the Irish Nationalists led by Charles Stewart Parnell. Faced with yet another revolt throughout Ireland, the Liberal government of the time passed the Irish Land Act of 1881 which gave them security of tenure. It was a concept which appealed to the men from Skye.

The Battle of the Braes
Braes is a crofting township south of Portree. In 1881 the

14

crofters demanded from Lord MacDonald the return of grazing rights on nearby Ben Lee. They refused to pay rent until this was done. An attempt to evict the ringleaders resulted in sheriffs officers being jostled and the eviction notices being burned, a routine response in this situation. Police arrived from Glasgow and Inverness and arrested the men in a pre-dawn swoop. All hell broke loose as men, women and children, but mainly women, pelted the police with mud and stones. About a dozen policemen were injured as they drew their batons to fight their way back to Portree with the prisoners.

Braes was the spark which lit the fire. Similar revolts broke out all over Skye, notably in Glendale, and soon spread across the Minch to Lewis. Sheep farms were occupied, fences torn down, sheep were eaten and crofters refused to pay rent. While the mainland was fairly quiet, disturbances of a lesser nature occurred in Tiree, Uist and Harris. Highland people had often attempted to resist eviction in the past, but their revolts had been confined to one place and were thus easily crushed. This was the biggest Highland revolt since 1745.

Most worrying to the landowners was the emergence of strong and determined leaders from among the crofters themselves. John MacPherson, a Skyeman, did not seem to respond to the traditional forms of intimidation. A spell in jail for grazing his cattle on the laird's land simply turned him into a martyr and celebrity. His friend, the Rev. Donald MacCallum was censured by the Church for inciting violence and class hatred. The poetry and songs of Mary MacPherson, Mairi Mhor nan oran (big Mary of the

songs), added powerful emotional fuel to the conflict. The Battle of the Braes was widely reported in national and local papers such as the pro-crofter *Oban Times*, winning valuable sympathy for the crofters' cause. In 1883 the Highland Land Law Reform Association was formed by prominent and successful Gaels mainly living in the cities of the south. It is usually known as the Land League. Its President was D H MacFarlane, a Highlander who became an Irish Nationalist MP before returning to win Argyll as a crofters' candidate in the election of 1885. Also prominent were Dr Roderick MacDonald from London, Alexander MacKenzie a Gaelic language activist and publisher from Inverness, John Stuart Blackie, a Professor of Greek who had taught himself Gaelic and two liberal MPs, Charles Fraser-MacIntosh (Inverness Burgh) and Dr Charles Cameron (Glasgow).

The Land League quickly developed a formidable local branch structure and a mass following in the Highlands and Islands. Its slogan 'Is treasa tuath na tighearna'—the people are mightier than a lord—had a ring of truth when spoken by people like John MacPherson.

The Napier Commission 1883

Worried by the disturbances and fearful that the Highlands would degenerate into violence and lawlessness, the government appointed Lord Napier, a judge and Lowland landowner, to head a Royal Commission to investigate the situation. There were no crofters on the commission but there were three landowners, Donald Cameron of Locheil, Charles Fraser-MacIntosh and Kenneth MacKenzie of Gairloch, all of whom had a reputation for

being sypmathetic to the crofters' cause. Also on the commission were Sheriff Alexander Nicholson, a Skyeman, and Professor Donald MacKinnon of Edinburgh University. All had good Gaelic except Napier and Locheil. They travelled all round the Highlands collecting evidence and listening to the submissions of peasants and factors alike, in Gaelic and in English. Their recommendations to the government formed the basis of the Crofters Act of 1886.

How successful, then, was this Act in dealing with the Highland problem?

1   The new law meant that crofters could no longer be evicted. However, they did not get back any of the land they had lost earlier and therefore they were condemned to continue to live in poverty. Emigration continued as before, leaving behind an increasingly aged population and weakening the indigenous culture of the region. There were small victories. In 1887 the new Land Court decided that Ben Lee belonged to the Braes people. Mairi Mhor wrote a song about it, Oran Beinn Li.

2   The great deer and sheep estates continued. In large numbers these animals do a huge amount of damage. Their grazing prevents the regrowth of native woodlands and causes deforestation. It also makes the soil acid and encourages bracken to grow everywhere. Victorian hunters shot not only deer and grouse, but almost anything else that moved as well. The Glen Garry game book for 1837 to 1840 records the destruction of the following 'vermin': " 27 white tailed eagles, 15 golden eagles,

18 ospreys, 63 goshawks, 285 common buzzards, 375 rough legged buzzards, 63 hen harriers, 78 merlins…". Thus white tailed eagles, ospreys, sea eagles and red kites were eliminated from the Highlands at that time and several other species, notably otters, pine martens, badgers, wild cats and golden eagles came close to extinction. Gaelic poetry of this period often uses the word 'fasach' (desert) to describe the results of the clearances. The 1886 Act did not reverse this environmental disaster.

3 It has sometimes been suggested that the Crofters Act was an attempt firstly to quieten the revolt while giving the crofters the minimum possible and secondly to break the unity which threatened the control of the landlords.

If this was the aim it succeeded. Land raids continued for many years, especially in Lewis. Some were successful; most were not. In 1887, 700 men with 57 rifles invaded the Pairc Deer forest in Lewis and shot over 100 deer which they took home to eat. Witnesses said that many of those involved were mainly interested in feeding their families. The police and army were called and the raiders withdrew. After the First World War, many returning servicemen hoped that, having fought for their country, they might be given a little bit of it. After intense agitation for new crofts to be created from the deer estates and sheep walks, the government bought about 100,000 hectares of land for this purpose. 1,500 crofters now occupy this land. It went a small way towards reversing the trend of the previous 150 years. One of the last land raids was in

Knoydart in 1948 when Lord Brocket, a neo-Nazi who had visited Hitler before the war, secured the legal removal of seven ex-servicemen who had tried to reclaim crofts from his Lordship's land. Knoydart has been sold several time since then and today there are no people of local origin living there.

IMMIGRATION TO SCOTLAND

During the 18th, 19th and 20th centuries, when Scots were leaving their homeland by the thousand, there were, nevertheless, people arriving here from other parts of Europe.

Irish Immigration

Links between Scotland and Ireland are very old. The Gaelic of South Argyll is very similar to the Gaelic of Donegal as the two areas are separated only by a short sea crossing and there has been an intermingling of the people since time immemorial. In the 1700s Irish people used to migrate seasonally to help with farm work in the south west. They were especially useful at harvest time when there was a great deal to be done in a very short time. High rents and terrible poverty at home drove them to migrate.

A number of key features distinguished Irish workers:

1 A willingness to work for lower wages than even the Highlanders would accept.

2 A willingness to do dirty or unpleasant work that nobody else wanted. In 1833, 350 out of 400 sugar workers in Greenock were Irish. One manufacturer said, "The Scotch would not work in sugar houses…If it were not for the Irish we

would be forced to give up trade…The Highlanders would not do the work."
(Report on Manufactures, Commerce & Shipping. (1833) quoted by D F MacDonald in Scotland's Shifting Population.)

3 An ability to look after themselves and each other. Large numbers of Irish labourers, or navvies, worked on the construction of canals in Scotland and England in the 1700s and railways in the 1800s. Many of them found work in the coal mines of west central Scotland, although very few worked in the Lothian and Fife coalfields.

Many Irish people were skilled textile workers with experience in the linen trade. They settled in places like Paisley, Lanark, Glasgow and Dundee where they got jobs in similar trades. In 1830 there were already 30,000 Irish people in Glasgow. The 1841 census shows that there were about 125,000 people of Irish birth in Scotland. In 1851, 12% of the population of the ten biggest Scottish towns was of Irish origin, the proportion being especially high in Dundee (19%) and Glasgow (18.2%). During the potato famine a million Irish people are believed to have died of starvation and a million more to have emigrated. At one point in 1848 they were reaching Glasgow at a rate of 1,000 per week. Many, however, were only passing through and after 1850 America became the main destination for Irish migrants.

Although Irish people settled in large numbers in Liverpool and London (and worked at building the English railway network) they never made up such a large part of the population of England. In 1861 almost 7% of Scotland's population was Irish born while in England the proportion was only 3%.

The Irish Influence on Scotland

Native Scots resented the Irish and accused them of dragging down wages. While this was undoubtedly true, it has to be counterbalanced by acknowledging their huge achievements in railway and canal construction, and their contribution to the wealth and success of Scottish industry. By 1880 they were becoming prominent in Trade Unions and were helping to push up wages. The arrival of large numbers of desperately poor people did nothing to ease the already impossible housing situation.

Religious tolerance had never been a strong point in Lowland Scotland and Irish immigration made the situation worse. Most of those who came before 1850 were Catholics from the south or Donegal. After 1870 large numbers of Protestants arrived from Ulster (Northern Ireland) to work in the Glasgow shipyards. The two Irish factions had a long tradition of mutual hatred in which local Scots were only too willing to join. Glasgow rapidly became a city divided by sectarian hatred. Protestants staged Orange Order marches through Glasgow and street violence became common.

Town	Protestant Team	Catholic Team
Glasgow	Rangers	Celtic
Edinburgh	Hearts	Hibernian
Dundee	Dundee	Dundee Utd.
Liverpool	Everton	Liverpool

The railways enabled sport to be organised and run on a national basis. Irish Catholics either started their own football teams or else concentrated their support on one particular team in a town. The Protestants did the same. Dundee United was initially called Dundee Hibernian, Hibernia being the Latin name for Ireland. Football matches formed a convenient focus for riots as rival supporters fought each other in the name of the Prince of Peace.

Religious discrimination also entered the work place. It was impossible for a Catholic to get a job in certain Clydeside shipyards.

Jews, Lithuanians and Italians

At the end of the 19th century Scotland received a sprinkling of migrants from other parts of Europe. Jews arrived to escape anti-semitism in Europe, especially in Russia where a vicious programme called the pogroms was designed to kill one-third of the Jewish population and oblige another third to emigrate. Italians arrived seeking greater prosperity than was possible at home. Many established cafes and chip shops.

Lithuanians came from the eastern Baltic, again in search of greater prosperity. Many settled near Bellshill in Lanarkshire and got work in the local iron industry. It is perhaps fortunate that none of these felt the need to start football teams, although a little Italian influence might have been no bad thing for the Scottish game.

EVALUATION EXERCISE

population change
in Scotland

The following activities refer to the information given on pages 3—6 and Source A.

Source A was written by Sir John Sinclair of Ulbster in 1825. Sir John was responsible for persuading all the ministers in Scotland to write an account of their parishes. These were collected together and published in various volumes between about 1790 and 1800. The collection is known as *The Old Statistical Account* and is very important evidence about Scotland's past. In 1825 he wrote the *Analysis of the Statistical Account,* some of which is quoted below. To start with he was writing about reasons for population growth (and) causes of decreased population (in some areas).

Reasons for population growth

* The beneficial effect of inoculation for the smallpox.
* The improvement of wastelands.
* Better cultivated soil, a more extensive employment of fishing.
* The great increase in manufactures.

(From *Analysis of the Statistical Account,* quoted by S Wood in *Changing Lives.*)

Reasons for population decrease

* The increased size of farms... There are numerous instances of one person renting a property in the cultivation of which six, eight or ten farmers had formerly been employed.
* The conversion of large tracts of the country into sheep farms. What can be more painful than to see one person living on a property on which formerly 100 inhabitants found a comfortable subsistence?
* Some of the modern improvements in agriculture.
* The habits of the lower ranks which make them afraid of marriage and desirous of enjoying the pleasures without the burdens of matrimony.
* The army and navy carry away numbers of young men.
* The flower of our young men incited by the prospect of making a fortune go abroad.

Questions

1 How useful is the cartoon *A Court for King Cholera* on page 5 as evidence about living conditions in British towns round about 1850?

2 How accurate is it about the cause of cholera?

3 Look at the picture of an operation on page 6. Is this a good source of information about Victorian medicine?

4 What does the picture tell us about Victorian hospitals?

5 Read Source A. Bearing in mind when it was written, how complete an account does this source give us of the reasons for population change?

6 How can you tell from the source to which social class Sir John belonged?

EVALUATION EXERCISE

the highland clearances

The following activities refer to information contained in Sources B – I.

Source B: Lord Strath Naver, a descendant of the Countess of Sutherland speaking to Dr J Hunter on a BBC schools TV programme around 1992.

> The people who lived on the estate ... were really in the process of slowly starving to death and were living in disgraceful conditions, conditions which no civilised person could have supported, and which certainly would not be tolerated for half a second today.
>
> ... people ... have passed on in legend a situation where the land was flowing with milk and honey and everything was fine and the wicked landowner came along and kicked them all out. Well that didn't happen—it wasn't like that.
>
> There were strong, solid, altruistic* reasons for doing what they did ... They did not want a single person to leave the county ...
>
> (*altruistic = considering the best interests of other people.)

Source C: Donald MacLeod, evicted from Strath Naver in 1819, wrote in his book, *Gloomy Memories*

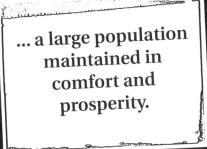

... a large population maintained in comfort and prosperity.

Source D was written by Sir John Sinclair of Ulbster, a Caithness landowner and government Minister who persuaded all the parish ministers of Scotland to submit an account of their parishes to what is now called the *Old Statistical Account*, published about 1795. Here he was writing in 1825 in the *Analysis of the Statistical Account* about the reasons for depopulation.

The conversion of large tracts of the country into sheep farms. What can be more painful than to see one person living on a property on which formerly 100 inhabitants found a comfortable subsistence?

Questions

1 What are the strengths and weaknesses of sources B–D as evidence about the Highland Clearances?

2 Describe the standpoint of each of the authors.

... Many tenants were unable to pay their rents so the landowner himself was in danger of getting into debt, for example, Lord MacDonald in Skye. ... migration was an attractive solution. Landowners could not give handouts of money or oats indefinitely.

Source E is from *Revise Your 'S' Grade History* by Rigg, Teale and Mackay. *The Case for the Landowner.*

The district of Croick is held by seven heritors or proprietors, whose total income, or rental derived from it is about £2,000 a year. Among the Highland population of 370 souls … about 27 were paupers … The voluntary assessment, or subscription of the seven heritors, as their share towards the support of the poor, 'the aged and feeble' of their own community, was—nothing. THEY NEVER GAVE A FAR-THING. The poor supported their own helpless poor; …

The parish of Assynt is in Sutherland,

adjoining this neighbourhood. The Duke of Sutherland is the sole heritor of the parish and derives a rental from it of about £3,000 a year; his subscription to the poor fund of the whole parish is £6 a year.

I am informed by a gentleman who knows Ross-shire well that many of the heritors and large farmers, having been led into expensive habits from the higher rents and prices obtained during the war, and not having been able to shake off these habits … are greatly shackled by debts and expenses.

Source F is from *The Times*, Wednesday 21 May, 1845. It appeared under the by-line 'from our own correspondent' and was about the clearance which was about to take place in Glen Calvie.

Source G is a translation (Cameron 1995) of a passage from Alexander Carmichael's *Carmina Gadelica* in which Catherine MacPhee of South Uist gave an eye witness account of an 1848 clearance. Her account was written down in the 1880s and was used by Run Rig in a song *Fichead Bliadhna* (20 Years).

Questions

1 To what extent do the writers of sources E and F agree on the landlords' justification for evicting their tenants?

2 Which of these sources do you think is most likely to be reliable? Give reasons for your answer.

3 How useful is source G as evidence of the alleged brutality of the clearances?

4 How much help do sources G, H and I give us in assessing why people emigrated to Canada in the mid-19th century?

Many things I have seen in my day and in my genera-tion. I saw the wives putting the chil-dren in the carts that were to put them from Iochdar and Beinn Bhladha. The married men tied beside them, unable to help them. I saw the big, strong men, heroes of the world, tied up on the quay at Loch Boisdale and thrown in the ship like cattle. They all left for the streets of Glasgow and the deserts of Canada, such of them who did not die of hun-ger or plague going across the ocean. The God of life and he only knows the vile work of men that day.

Source H and Source I are fragments of Gaelic songs written in Canada.

Source H: This is from a song in praise of Cape Breton. Attributed to a MacDonald from Uist, it starts

"Salainn an t-aite th'agam ri taobh na traghad"
(Lovely is the place I have beside the beach)

Source I: *O Mo Dhuthaich* (*Oh my country)* was written by Alan MacPhee from Uist while living in Manitoba, Canada.

Thig iad ugainn, carach, seolta
Gus ar meallach far ar n-eolais
Molaidh iad dhuinn Manitoba
Duthaich fhuar, gun ghual, gun mhoine.

They will come to us, cunning and wily
in order to entice us from our homes
They will praise Manitoba to us
A cold land without coal, without peat.

Gaelic lyrics and translation taken from the Capercaillie CD *The Blood is Strong*.
According to tradition Alan MacPhee eventually managed to get enough money together to return to South Uist.

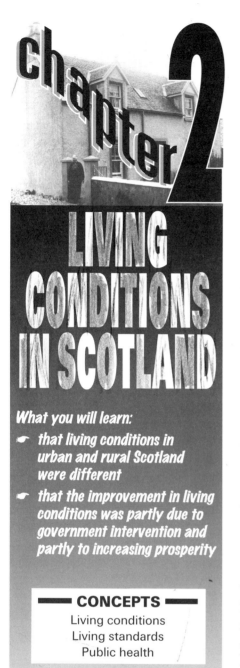

chapter 2

LIVING CONDITIONS IN SCOTLAND

What you will learn:

- ☛ that living conditions in urban and rural Scotland were different
- ☛ that the improvement in living conditions was partly due to government intervention and partly to increasing prosperity

---
CONCEPTS

Living conditions
Living standards
Public health

THE TERM 'living conditions' is used when we describe people's immediate environment. It is concerned with the quality of housing. Were the houses well built, dry, warm, comfortable and well ventilated? Was there enough space inside for the occupants? Did they have access to clean water and effective sanitation? 'Living conditions' also covers the immediate surroundings of the houses—for instance whether the streets were clean or a hazard to health.

Living standards in Scotland improved considerably during the period we are studying. Throughout this time they depended greatly on the wealth of the family concerned and, to some extent, where they lived. There were important differences between town and country, Highlands, Islands and Lowlands.

RURAL LIVING CONDITIONS

The Highlands and Islands

In speaking about rural housing in the Highlands we need to avoid overgeneralisation. Houses varied in style and construction from one part of the area to another. In 1830 some of the poorest people still lived in houses whose walls were made from turf, cut from the ground and laid flat, layer on layer, to make the walls. In the outer islands most of the houses were stone and built to a design said to have been inherited from the Vikings. The name 'taigh dubh' (tie-ee doo) or black house has been given to this style of house.

A typical Hebridean black house is shown below. A long, low building, it had no windows. The walls were rarely more than 1.8 metres high and were made from rough stone, cleverly fitted together without cement. There was an inner and an outer wall with the space between filled with sand or soil, the top being sealed with clay. The corners were rounded off and the roof rested on the inner wall. The rafters were made from driftwood or even whale bones collected from the beach as wood was scarce in the Islands. The heather thatch was tied down with ropes and stones to stop it blowing away.

The living space within the house was not usually divided by

Long Island Type of House (Black House)

General View

Construction Detail

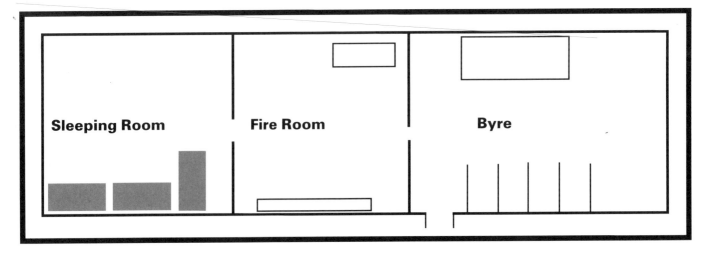

| Sleeping Room | Fire Room | Byre |

internal walls, but typically there would be three main areas as illustrated above.

The cattle were kept at one end in what would be called 'the byre' in Scots or 'a' bhathach' (uh vaa-uch) in Gaelic. The cattle used the same door as the people and traditionally the dung was only removed in the spring when 30 to 50 tons would be removed and spread on the fields. A sanitary inspector said, in 1897, "One would imagine from the care bestowed on the dung that it ... was the most valuable asset the people possessed. It must, on no account be placed outside for fear of being washed away by rain". When

A Landowner's home. Achnacarry, completed in the 1830s, home of the Camerons of Locheil; photographed in 1897 on the 21st birthday of Donald Walter Cameron of Locheil seen on the right with his parents. Donald Walter led the Cameron Highlanders during the First World War until he was invalided out. Two of his three brothers were killed in the War. His father, Donald Cameron, was one of the commissioners on the Napier Commission which looked into the problems of crofting. Also seen in the photograph are some of the estate workers, tenants and crofters. Achnacarry was used as a training base for the commandos, Britain's elite special forces, during the Second World War.

the same gentleman suggested that they should not have cows in the house he was "solemnly told that without the company of the inhabitants the poor beasts would be homesick".

In the centre of the house was the living area, known as 'aig an teine' (ayk an tyena) which literally means 'at the fire'. A peat fire burned continuously in the middle of the floor. There was no chimney and the smoke found its way out through a hole in the thatch, through the thatch itself or through the door. To avoid breathing in the smoke it was necessary to sit or crouch down. The soot built up under the thatch, hanging down in what looked like long, trailing cobwebs. In the spring these were removed and put on the fields, along with the dung and seaweed from the shore. Sometimes the entire heather thatch was spread on the land. Agricultural historians have never given these people the credit they deserve for the efforts they made to preserve and improve their land.

During heavy rain sooty drips often fell on the people, their food and their possessions. Babies' cradles had a hood to keep the drips off their faces. In some islands such as North Ronaldsay and Sanday in Orkney, Heiskir, Muck, Canna and Tiree there

Valtos, Isle of Lewis 1938.

was no peat. The people were forced to burn a mixture of dried seaweed, cow dung and horse dung to survive.

The house frequently had an earth floor which would probably be damp. Furniture was sparse. There would be one or two 'cistes'—chests for clothes, meal, potatoes or blankets. A few simple seats, stools and a dresser would be made from driftwood.

At the end of the house, opposite the byre, was 'uachdar an taighe' (ooachkar an tyuh), the top of the house, the posh room. It would contain box beds which might make the partition with the living area, a big ciste for blankets, a spinning wheel and perhaps little else. The house had no lavatory. Usually there was a little house, 'taigh beag'

(tie-ee bake) outside. Human excrement was collected and it went on the fields along with the cow dung, the soot and the seaweed.

The black house obviously contained some health hazards. Living with the cattle posed the threat of bovine tuberculosis, which is less serious and more difficult to contract than the human form.

They also suffered from stomach upsets and enteritis, known locally as dung fever. The smoke from the fire was bad for the lungs and could cause bronchitis. Tuberculosis was unusually common in the Highlands and in Ireland at that time. The people of these areas may have had a low resistance to it, perhaps because it had only re-

House Typical of Eastern & Central Highlands

General View

Construction Detail

Improved croft house. Croft 47, Banavie, Inverness-shire. c 1890—1900

cently been introduced to the area by returning migrants. TB, a then lethal lung disease, is spread by a bacillus which thrives in damp, poorly ventilated houses and the black house had an earth floor and no windows. The people were reluctant to accept that their homes were health hazards. In June 1897 the *Inverness Courier* reported a speech by William MacKenzie, sanitary inspector for Ross and Cromarty. "...The inhabitants were, as a class, strong and able-bodied fellows. Indeed they are well above average in this respect, notwithstanding their insanitary state, and they continually taunted him with this when he discussed matters with them. If he wanted to see weakly, insignificant looking men, they said, he had better go to his own country... Infant mortality was high, but strange to say, general mortality was not high."

On the mainland, the ready availability of wood and greater shelter from the wind made it possible for people to build higher houses with steeper roofs. In the southern Highlands and Argyll the cottages were square, rather than having the streamlined rounded corners of island houses.

Orkney long houses were similar in design to Lewis houses because of their common Viking ancestry. The Orkney houses, however, often had roofs made from large flat flagstones which were quarried on the islands and which conveniently broke off in flat slabs.

As the century progressed a new type of house began to appear. These were copies of the houses which were built for shepherds on the big sheep estates. They had squared corners, walls built with some dressed stone and mortar and a roof of slate, thatch

or after 1830, corrugated iron. Sometimes these were extended by the addition of an upper storey or a kitchen extension behind. They came to be known as 'taighean geala' (tie-an gyalluh) or white houses. Not only did they have windows but they also had glass in these windows. The floor would be of wood or stone. There were fireplaces and chimneys and often a black, cast iron range or stove on which to cook. These houses are an indication of the greater prosperity and rising living standards which were experienced throughout Scotland after 1850. Those who could not afford a white house, or who disliked the new ways, modified the black house, adding floors, windows and chimneys. Seamen and herring girls returning home brought treasures with them—a big clock from America, a dresser from Glasgow or a tea-set with 'a present from Yarmouth' printed on each cup or plate. The Crofters Act of 1886 gave them a great incentive to improve their homes since they were no longer in danger of being evicted and losing their investment.

The photograph on page 24 shows an improved croft house on croft 47, Banavie, near Fort William. It began as a two room, stone cottage about 1840 when the family was evicted from a remote glen and was resettled here. The second storey of two bedrooms was added in 1889, only three years after the Crofters Act. Other improvements at this time included piped water from a dam on the hill, a flush toilet and a septic tank. Few crofters could afford improvements on this scale. Typically they were made possible by the fact that the crofter's husband was a sea captain.

Large-scale farmers in the Highlands usually had substantial two storey houses with good slate roofs. Landowners vied with each other to build more and more ostentatious mansions or 'castles', with huge numbers of rooms and servants quarters. The costs involved often contributed to the bankruptcy of the owner and the sale of the estate.

LOWLAND SCOTLAND AND URBAN LIVING

Lowland Scotland contains a number of distinct regions. However, by 1830 Central Scotland, the Border counties, and the North-Eastern coastal plain (stretching from Dundee, past Aberdeen, round to Inverness and beyond to the Dornoch Firth), had experienced an 'agricultural revolution' which gave rise to fairly uniform housing conditions.

Landowners, the rural elite, had their mansions and castles. They

were much less prone to bankruptcy than their Highland counterparts. Farmers who rented or owned farms could expect, by 1830, to live in large, substantial stone houses.

At this time large arable farms might employ upwards of 30 workers. The unmarried men would live together in mutual squalor in a hovel called 'the bothy'. Here they cooked over an open fire, ate and slept. Sometimes the horsemen lived in a room above the stables. Unmarried women often lived in attic rooms in the farmhouse itself. Married workers usually lived in farm cottages, many of which possessed the less attractive features of Highland black houses—earth floors, few windows and a turf roof. By 1870 farmers were finding it hard to compete for labour with growing industries and higher wages in the towns. They were forced to provide better housing. Rows of reasonably solid stone or brick cottages appeared on every farm. They would have stone or wooden floors, a fireplace and, by the end of the century, running water. It was well into the twentieth century before the majority of these had flush toilets and septic tanks to digest the sewage.

Living Conditions in the Towns and Cities

Scottish towns were among the filthiest in Europe before the industrial revolution. In the 17th and even the 18th centuries the good people of Edinburgh were well known for emptying buckets of excrement and household rubbish out of their windows into the street below. The more considerate of them would shout 'Gardyloo' in warning to those below. 'Gardyloo' comes from the French 'Gardez l'eau', beware of water! This colourful habit had largely ceased by 1830

and a system whereby sewage was removed from the town in 'nightsoil carts' was enforced to some extent. Despite this the streets were still filthy. Although even the wealthiest people were not immune to these problems, the situation was worst for the poorest town dwellers. The main problems were as follows.

Overcrowding

Scotland's manufacturing industries expanded rapidly after 1760. Large numbers of people were attracted to towns like Glasgow, Greenock, Motherwell, Falkirk, Dundee, Galashiels, Hawick and many others. They came from the surrounding countryside, from Ireland and from the Highlands. A severe housing shortage occurred. Table 2.1 gives some idea of the scale of the problem.

In some areas wealthy people abandoned the town centre and moved to better houses on the outskirts, encouraged, after 1840 by good railway links. The houses they left behind were divided up and became home to many poor families who often live one family to a room. Thus Gorbals, once home to Glasgow's finest, became a slum of international notoriety.

In most towns business people put up cheap housing to rent to the desperate. Generally 'tenements', blocks of flats 3 or 4 storeys high, were the style most favoured in Scotland. 'Closes' often ran through the tenement blocks to give access to a courtyard beyond where people dried their washing and dumped ashes and rubbish on a midden heap. Here also would be found their 'dry lavatories'. As Table 2.2 shows Census evidence illustrates that few families had much living space. Things did improve, if slowly. The housing situation in Scotland was worse

Scotland's Urban Population

	1841	1911
Glasgow	275,000	784,000
Edinburgh & Leith	164,000	401,000
Dundee	60,000	165,000
Aberdeen	65,000	164,000

If the populations of nearby Govan and Partick were added to Glasgow's the 1911 figure would exceed one million.

Table 2.1   **Source:** From *A Century of the Scottish People* by T C Smout.

than that in England and Wales. In 1911 Glasgow had 66% of its population living in one or two roomed homes whereas the figure for Scotland as a whole was 50% with 7% for England and Wales. In Glasgow single roomed homes were called 'single ends'. The tenement house did have certain advantages for the poor who had to live there. With neighbours above and below and perhaps on three sides, heat was shared and retained so that the room was cheap to heat. Also, only one room had to be lit. When flush lavatories were introduced late in the 19th century they often took the form of stairhead toilets built on each landing of the tenement and shared by perhaps four or more families. With 20 or more people sharing one lavatory queues were a problem, but nobody had to endure the agony of a cold seat.

The disadvantages of one or two roomed homes are not hard to see. There was no privacy for anybody and it was impossible to get away from the rest of the family when a quarrel was in progress.

In 1861 10% of all single ends had no windows. In these conditions diseases passed quickly from one person to another, especially TB, which thrives in conditions of poor ventilation and where the victim has to breath in the bacillus from an affected person.

Furnishings were, to say the least, sparse. A bed recess was often curtained off from the room. The parents would sleep here, and sometimes their children too. Straw mattresses might be put on the floor for the children and for the lodgers who were quite common, even in single ends. Not all houses had a

Close No. 80 High Street, Glasgow c 1868

Scottish Homes in 1861

35% had 1 room

37% had 2 rooms

11% had 3 rooms

17% had 4 or more rooms

Table 2.2
Source: *A Century of the Scottish People*. T C Smout.

table or chairs. In 1830 there would not be running water in the house. This would have to be carried up from a stand pipe or well. An open fire gave heat to the room and was essential for cooking.

Lack of Sanitation

There was no proper system of sewage removal. In many towns human excrement was mixed with animal dung and was flushed along open drains by rain water until it reached a river which was almost certainly being used as a source of drinking water.

In other places sewage was collected in deep pits, called cesspools, where it would gradually be consumed by bacteria. Sometimes contamination seeped from these cesspools through the ground-water into wells dug into the water-table. The results were unpleasant!

Clean drinking water was very rare. Private water companies sold people drinking water contaminated by their own filth. One private water supply company in Glasgow drew its water from the Clyde. In 1832, 1848, 1853 and 1867 there were severe outbreaks of cholera, a disease which arrived from India about 1820. It is contracted by drinking water contaminated by the excrement of a sufferer. Victims suffer severe dehydration caused by vomiting and constant diar-

Middle class homes. Montgomery Crescent, Glasgow

rhoea. Death from kidney failure was a common outcome. This scourge ravaged not only the towns and cities but country areas as well. Beside the village of Inver in Easter Ross a substantial mound is marked by a simple sign which you can read below.

While it was unusual for half the people of a settlement to die, death rates of 10 to 20% of a major settlement's population were common. In the 1853 outbreak 6,000 people died of cholera in Scotland, of whom 4,000 were in Glasgow. It was only in 1854 that John Snow, a London investigator, proved that cholera was caused by sewage contaminated drinking water after 500 residents of Soho died in one outbreak.

The Living Conditions of the Urban Poor

Closely related to the idea of 'living conditions' is the concept of 'living standards'. This measures the ability of people to get the essentials of life—food, clothing and shelter—for themselves and their families. In towns this depends entirely on how much money they can earn.

In 1901 Seebohm Rowntree published *Poverty: A Study of Town Life*. This was based on a systematic survey of the working people of York and revealed that 28% of the townsfolk, 43% of the

working class, lived below what he called the 'poverty line'. They did not earn enough to provide themselves with the minimum of food, clothes and shelter needed for a healthy life. This report shocked Britain because York was a prosperous city.

There was no shortage of evidence to show the effects of poverty in Scottish towns. Many photographs of this period show children suffering from rickets, a complaint common now in the Third World. A disease of malnutrition, it affects children with an inadequate diet. If they do not get enough calcium, their growing bones become soft and deformed. Bow legs are the obvious symptom. This disease probably became more common as the 19th century progressed. The poor switched from a diet of porridge and milk, potatoes and herring to one of bread and jam, tea and sugar with a little poor quality meat or broth from time to time. When the army organised mass recruiting for the First World War in 1914, it was amazed by the number of volunteers it had to reject as being physically unfit to die for King and Country. The problem of a sugar rich diet and poor teeth spread throughout Scotland, finally reaching the Hebrides and the Northern Isles in the 1920s.

Severe malnutrition was a prob-

Cumaibh an Inbhir Beo
'Let Inver Live'

Here in a mass grave lies half the population of the village of Inver who died during the cholera epidemic of 1832.

R.I.P.

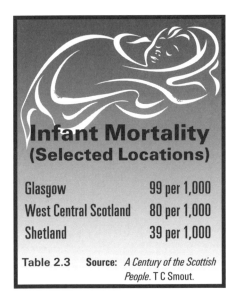

Infant Mortality
(Selected Locations)

Glasgow	99 per 1,000
West Central Scotland	80 per 1,000
Shetland	39 per 1,000

Table 2.3   Source: *A Century of the Scottish People*. T C Smout.

SOME CHANGES IN THE HOUSE

In 1848 electric light became available in London. However, many places in the Scottish Highlands did not get it until the 1950s.

A flushing lavatory had been invented as early as 1596, but during the 19th century most Scots continued to use dry lavatories or privvies. The flushing cistern seems to have been invented by a London plumber called Thomas Crapper round about 1872. After 1885 these were often linked to free-standing WC pedestals made by Twyfords. To begin with such luxuries would only be available to the rich, but as earnings increased in the 20th century more and more families were connected to the network.

Between 1820 and 1840, closed coal burning kitchen ranges began to replace open fires for cooking. These were made possible by the improved technology of iron and steel manufacture. They offered many of the amenities which we now take for granted— domestic hot water heated by a back boiler, ovens and a hot surface for heating pots

An early Twyford WC with siphonic cistern.

without turning them sooty black. Kitchen ranges eventually found their way into the homes not only of the rich but of tenement dwellers, farm workers and crofters.

In the 20th century they were gradually replaced by gas and electric cookers, although many rural Highland homes still had ranges in the 1950s. The 20th century has also seen the introduction of numerous electrical appliances. The first vacuum cleaners made their debut in the homes of the super-rich before the First World War.

---

lem of the towns. Rickets was virtually unknown in rural areas. In 1910, 9% of all Scottish school children suffered from this problem, but by 1950 improved living standards and social welfare had cut this figure to 0.3%. Infant mortality, the number of babies who die in their first year, can also be revealing. (See Table 2.3.)

The Living Conditions of the Urban Middle Classes

As one would expect, wealthy people had better homes. The coming of the railways enabled the more prosperous to leave the very smoky inner cities and settle downwind in the less polluted suburbs which sprang up on the edge of all major towns and cities. Large houses were built with servant accommodation in the attics and cellars.

The wealthy of Edinburgh began to abandon the old town, between the castle and Holyrood Palace, at the end of the 1700s. They moved into more spacious accommodation in the New Town, between Princes Street and Queen Street. Their new homes did not at first contain WCs, which were added after 1850. Many of the new houses had a tapped water supply.

Improvements in Living Conditions 1830–1930

British cities were so dangerously dirty and full of disease that even the government became concerned. Cholera was no respecter of rank and even rich people died. The outbreaks of 1832 and 1848 caused a degree of panic and a determina-

tion to do something about it, even though the causes of the disease were unknown at the time.

The favoured solution to all urban problems was to give powers to elected local councils and then leave them to get on with it. The basis of the system was the

Glasgow Corporation Housing. Red sandstone tenements at Anniesland Cross, Glasgow 1930s.

Burgh Reform Act of 1833.

The Burgh Reform Act 1833

Scottish burghs had had councils for centuries. They were controlled by the wealthiest traders and merchants. The 1833 Act said that they were to be elected by the £10 householders of the burgh. (All men owning or renting a house with an annual rental value of £10.) The council could act as 'Police Commissioners' and could collect a local tax called the rates similar to the present Council Tax. This money could be spent on keeping law and order and also on cleaning, paving and lighting the streets, rounding up beggars, naming streets and numbering houses in them. It was possible for Police Commissioners to be elected and to exist as a body separate from the Burgh Council.

A number of useful acts were passed in England, such as the Public Health Act of 1848 and the Sanitary Act of 1866 which gave English towns the right to provide sewers and clean water suplies. However, these did not apply in Scotland. Instead, Scotland had The Nuisance Removal Act 1855. Through this the Police Commissioners received additional powers to clean or close properties which were a threat to the health of the public.

1867 Public Health Act

This was a measure of great importance. Councils got powers to clean streets and houses, regulate boarding houses, provide hospitals and, of vital importance, lay drains and sewers. However, the councils were not compelled to do these things.

The Burgh Police (Scotland) Act 1892 and The Public Health (Scotland) Act 1897 made it compulsory for councils to make sanitary and building regula-

tions and to enforce them. During the 1800s many councils felt frustrated by their lack of power to change the situation. Their solution was to persuade their MPs to persuade Parliament to pass special laws giving them powers. Glasgow was notable in this respect. In 1855 Parliament was persuaded to pass the Glasgow Corporation Water Works Act. (Corporation was another name for city council.) This gave the city the right to turn Loch Katrine, 56 kilometres away in the Trossachs, into a reservoir to provide 50 million gallons of clean Highland water daily to people hitherto accustomed to drinking the River Clyde. When Queen Victoria opened the scheme in 1859 it had cost £1.5 million. Not to be outdone, Edinburgh arranged to use St Mary's Loch, high up in the Border hills. Soon every significant town in Scotland felt obliged to follow suit. When cholera broke out again in 1865, only 53 people died in Glasgow out of 400 in Scotland as a whole.

The latter part of the 19th century was a period of great civic pride in Glasgow as the 'City Fathers' took over or laid on a wide variety of utilities or services. In 1867 they took over the supply of gas from private enterprise, halving the price to the consumer. Gas street lighting was provided. A fire service was established, alongside municipal baths and wash-houses, a fever hospital, a municipal laundry, a telephone service and beautiful parks in which the residents could walk. The second city of the British Empire could scarcely have settled for less.

Housing

The provision of sewers and a clean water supply was achieved at great financial cost to the towns and cities. Yet the appall-

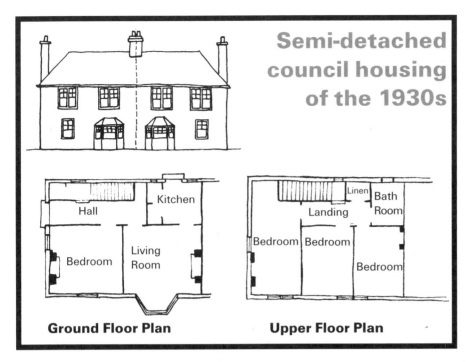

Semi-detached council housing of the 1930s

Hall

Kitchen

Bedroom

Living Room

Ground Floor Plan

Linen

Bath Room

Landing

Bedroom

Bedroom

Bedroom

Upper Floor Plan

ing state of housing meant that huge numbers of people were condemned to live in unbelievably dreadful conditions. In 1875 the Artisans and Labourers Dwellings Act gave councils the right to buy and demolish slum properties which they considered to be unhealthy. This may sound like progress, but it did not help the situation since the act did not provide for rebuilding. By 1885, 30,000 Glasgow people no longer had a slum to go home to because of this Act.

In 1888 the Corporation started to build replacements and by 1914 had completed 2,199 homes plus 78 'model lodging houses', housing in all 2% of the city's population. Most Scottish towns followed suit. The 1909 Housing Act, one of many reforms passed by the Liberal gov-

ernment of the time, gave councils the right to demolish and rebuild as they saw fit. When the First World War came to an end in 1918, there was a general mood in the country that the terrible sacrifices made in the previous four years had to mean something. People felt that if working men could be asked to die for Britain it was wrong to expect them to live in festering slums. David Lloyd George, the Prime Minister, sensed the mood of the time and pledged himself to build a "land fit for heroes" to live in.

Under the 1919 Housing Act (otherwise known as the Addison Act after Christopher Addison, the Minister of Health, who introduced it) councils were to survey their housing situation and draw up an action plan.

They were to raise money from the rates, the local tax, for house building. The government would pay for any cash shortfall. 25,540 good quality homes were built under this scheme—houses with up-market style facilities such as bathrooms, bedrooms and kitchens. The national economic situation became very difficult and the scheme was abandoned in 1921. The 1923 Housing Act was brought in by Neville Chamberlain, a Conservative with a long record of interest in working-class housing. A subsidy was offered to councils who built another 4,022 homes. Attractive subsidies to private builders saw the erection of an additional 30,000 private houses.

Britain got its first ever Labour government in 1924. It did not have a majority in Parliament and did not last long. John Wheatley, one of the famous radical MPs from 'red Clydeside' increased the subsidy offered by Chamberlain and although it was again reduced when Labour fell from office the same year, 75,000 homes were ultimately built under this scheme.

Council house building continued under one scheme or another until the Conservative election victory of 1979, by which time more than half of all Scottish families lived in council houses and the more gruesome features of Scottish urban housing had been removed.

EVALUATION EXERCISE
highland houses

The following activities refer to the information given in Sources A, B and C.

The old-fashioned Highland house was the essential setting for a ceilidh. The old houses were built for a different sort of life. They were evolved by a people of 'immense ability' to withstand the severe local conditions …They gave nightly warmth and shelter that was craved by men and women who spent their days largely out-of-doors,(and) had few worldly possessions.

Most 18th century travellers … found nothing to admire in our traditional houses. They were dismissed as dark and dirty and often referred to as huts. Seen from outside they were often likened to 'smoking dunghills'. Their interiors were said to be scenes of 'nastyness and simplicity'.

Am Fasgadh (The Highland Folk Museum, Kingussie) …is in a very cold district and in the severe winter of 1947 my own substantially built house was glacially cold every morning before the fire was lighted, whereas, if I lighted a fire in the eastern mainland cottage, an appreciable warmth remained for two or three days, and, in my reproduction of a Lewis cottage for a week.

Source C: From *Highland Folk Ways* (published 1961) by Dr Isabel Grant, a lady of immense scholarship with a great love of Highland people and their heritage.

Wonderful is the power of the affection which links human love to dark, dirty, turf huts with earthen floors and heather roofs, half kraals and half cowsheds! Let me frankly confess that, with the exception of one stone cottage, all the cabins I inspected filled me with disgust. It is disgraceful that human beings should pig in such places. The people are greatly to blame for their dirt, their slovenly habits and their indifference to improvements.

On entering one hovel, after picking my steps through the dunghill, I was met … by a cow's tail.

Source A: From *The Rosses of Glen Calvie* by John Robertson, written in 1845 as a protest against the eviction of the people of the glen.

Questions

1. To what extent do these two writers (Sources A and B) agree about the houses and living conditions of Glen Calvie people in 1845?

2. How might we explain any differences in the two accounts of the same houses?

3. Is Source C likely to be a reliable source of information on traditional Highland homes?

4. What sections in the passage indicate Dr Grant's affection for the people of the Highlands and their homes?

5. How complete an account of these homes does this extract give? You should use knowledge recalled from previous study of this topic.

6. Which of the two earlier sources, A and B, is closest to Dr Grant's opinions of traditional Highland homes? Justify your answer.

Source B: From *The Times* (London rather than Oban) whose 'own correspondent' was describing the same houses in May 1845.

The cottages themselves are outside apparently low heaps of turf. They are grown over so as to be of the colour of the brown hills, and at a distance are indistinguishable from the hill. They are all built on one plan and are divided into three compartments. The first you enter is a cowshed; a doorway out of this leads into the family room, and another doorway beyond leads to the far room, which is the bedroom and state apartment, being kept tidy and appropriated to receive visitors. The fire is on a stone in the middle of the family or centre room, and warms the whole cottage. Though the roof and sides are blackened with the peat smoke, everything within them is clean and orderly. And for what are these people to be reduced from comfort to beggary?

EVALUATION EXERCISE

living standards and conditions in urban Scotland

The following activities refer to the information given in Sources D—H.

Source D is from a report by Dr W L Lawrie to the Poor Law Commissioners about conditions in Greenock in 1842.

> The great proportion of the dwellings of the poor are situated in very narrow and confined closes or alleys …(which) … have little ventilation, the space between the houses being so narrow as to exclude the action of the sun on the ground …
>
> The 'lands' of houses which the poor inhabit are generally two or three storeys high, divided into flats, there being four or five families on each flat, … they possess one or two rooms each. … The average size of each room I should think would be from eight to nine feet square…
>
> From the high rent … a man with a large family … is unable to have more than one small room. I have found even two or three families inhabiting a room not large enough for the same number of individuals.
>
> There are … a good many lodging houses for vagrants. The charge for lodgings being 2d and 3d. 2d being the charge when more than two occupy the same bed.

Source E describes Glasgow in 1818 and was written by Dr Robert Graham. (From *Glasgow Observed* by Simon Berry and Hamish Whyte)

> If any man wonders at the prevalence of … fever, among the lower classes in Glasgow, … let him take the walk which I did today … Let him pick his steps among every species of disgusting filth, through an alley, from four to five feet wide, flanked by houses five floors high. …We found in one lodging house, fifteen feet long, by nine feet from the front of the beds to the opposite wall; that fifteen people were sometimes accommodated … The woman of the house … said … that each family was provided with a bed and that she very seldom had anybody lying on the floor.

Source F is also from Dr Lawrie's 1842 report on Greenock.

> In those closes where there is no dunghill the excrement and other offensive matter is thrown into the gutter before the door or carried out and put in the street … In nearly every close there is a dunghill, seldom or never covered in; few of these are cleaned out above once or twice a year; most of them are emptied when they can hold no more: to some of these privies are attached, and one privy serves a whole neighbourhood … Behind my consulting room, where I am now sitting, there is a large dunghill with a privy attached; to my knowledge that privy has not been emptied for six months; it serves a whole neighbourhood, and the effluvium is so offensive that I cannot open the window.

Source G is from a report by Dr Robert Sutherland about measures to deal with cholera in Glasgow in 1848–49. (From *Glasgow Observed* by Simon Berry and Hamish Whyte)

There are large square midden steads, some of them actually under the houses, and all of them in the immediate vicinity of the windows and doors of human dwellings. These receptacles hold the entire filth and offal of large masses of people and households, until country farmers can be bargained with for their removal.

Source H comes from a *Report on the Pollution of the River Clyde for the Health Committee of the Police Board* (1874). (From *Glasgow Observed* by Simon Berry and Hamish Whyte)

Main sewers and natural streams within the city boundary—now all used for drainage purposes—measuring together very nearly one hundred miles, receive and convey ... through the City sewage from 101,368 dwelling houses, and from sale-shops, warehouses, manufactories, and work-shops, numbering in the aggregate 16,218; including 31,927 water closets, 71,291 sinks, 3,865 fixed basins, and urine from 121 urinals, 5,288 ashpits, 935 privies, 2,304 stables, and 311 cow-houses, and discharge the same direct into the Clyde from 42 outlets ... In addition to the latter ... 20 manufactories discharge their waste outflow by private drains direct into the Clyde.

uestions

1   What purpose do you think the authors had in mind when they wrote these passages? Explain your answer.

2   Could the 'purpose' of the writers reduce the reliablity of their work as historical sources?

3   In what ways do sources D and E and the photograph of tenement housing on page 26 agree about housing conditions in urban Scotland in the first half of the 19th century?

4   Is it possible to get a balanced view of urban housing at this time from these sources?

5   Compare the plan of a council house in the 1930's on page 30 with sources D and E. How complete an account do these sources give of the progress made between 1840 and 1930?

6   Is Source F likely to be a reliable source about urban hygiene in 1840? Do you think it might be exaggerated? Give reasons for your answer.

7   How far do sources F and G support the view that hygiene was generally a problem in Scottish towns in 1840?

8   Does Source H contain any evidence of improvement in Glasgow between the time Dr Sutherland wrote his report in 1848–49 (Source G), and 1874 , when source H was published?

9   In what respect was the situation still unsatisfactory?

chapter 3

LIVING & WORKING ON THE LAND

What you will learn:

- ☞ *that Scottish agriculture changed quickly*
- ☞ *that the work and the way of life of Scottish agricultural workers did not change greatly*
- ☞ *that changes overseas had a dramatic effect on agriculture in Scotland*
- ☞ *that trade unions were not very successful in agriculture*
- ☞ *that government actions had good and bad effects on Scottish agriculture*

— CONCEPTS —
Bondagers
Migrant Labour
Trade Unionism
Economic Fluctuation
Mechanisation

Extract From Census For Fans Farm, Earlston, Berwickshire, 1881

House	Number of Houses	NAME and Surname of each person	Occupation	County of Birth
Fans Farm	1	Robert Hunter Herbertson	Head. Married. Farmer of 1343 acres of which 1050 arable. Employing 22 men, 16 women and 2 boys.	Galashiels
		Janet do.	Wife. Married. Farmers wife.	Earlston
		Bessie do.	Daughter	Selkirk
		Effie Hunter do.	Daughter	Earlston
		William Johnstone	Visitor. Unmarried. Seed merchant.	Earlston
		Richard Wade	Visitor. Unmarried. Commercial traveller.	Leith
		Maggie Riddell	Servant. Unmarried. General Servant (Domestic).	Selkirkshire
		Maggie Dalgleish	Servant. Unmarried. Nurse	Roxburghshire
Fans Farm	1	Charlie Scott	Head. Married. Shepherd.	Cranshaws
		Elizabeth Scott	Wife. Married.	Duns
		John Murray	Boarder. Unmarried. Assistant shepherd.	Hawick

Source: Census 1881

Women farmworkers or 'bondagers' in East Lothian

I N 1830 agriculture was the most important industry in Scotland. More than 60% of the population of Scotland earned a living from working on the land. The vast majority of land in Scotland was owned by the great landowners like the Duke of Buccleuch, the Duke of Sutherland and the Marquis of Breadalbane. These men ran huge estates and rented out portions of their land. In earlier times the land had been rented out to village communities or farm towns but in the 1700s, during the agricultural revolution, the land had been cleared of the village communities and farms had been created which were let out to individual tenants. In a very few cases the farm towns survived right through to the twentieth century, one particularly good example being Auchindrain, near Inveraray in Argyll on the West coast.

Running the Estates

The person who ran the estate was the factor or the landowner's agent. Since many of the landowners did not live permanently on their estates, the role of the factor was a very important one. He was not always a popular figure, since he had it in his power to renew leases or otherwise, and he often had different interests from the tenants.

As well as controlling the tenant farmers, the estate factor could oversee other rural industries which were part of the work of the estate. These might include a gamekeeper, a sawmiller, a forester, a joiner, a fox hunter, a mason, a deerstalker, a ghillie etc. In fact, the estates were often almost self-sufficient communities. By 1830 they were seen as moneymaking businesses by their owners.

By far the most important aspect of the estate was agriculture. For this purpose the estate land was broken down into farms which could be managed by one person. Sometimes the estate would keep some of the farms and would appoint a manager to run them. However, it was much more usual to lease out the farms to tenant farmers for a fixed period. By 1830 it had been recognised that the longer the lease the better, since that encouraged the tenant farmer both to invest money in improving his land and to manage it sensibly. The tenant would not expect to run the farm by himself. There was little machinery in use in 1830 so agriculture was very labour intensive. In other words, it required a great many people to do the work. The size of the farm varied from estate to estate and also depended on the quality of the land available. For example, a farm of 50–100 acres in arable Lowland Scotland was just as good as one of 1,000 acres of mountain in the Highlands. In each case the farmer would appoint staff to do the work.

The Farm Workers
The number of farm workers or hinds could be very large indeed— sometimes almost as many farm workers as had lived in the farm town. Farm workers

Killing and butchering a pig at Greenlaw, Berwickshire

were engaged for a six month term of work, the terms starting in November and May. It was quite usual to move to another job after the six month term and it was quite unusual to settle in a farm for much more than two or three years. The farm workers would negotiate a pay rate with the farmer at the start of the term. Often the details of this agreement would be kept as a secret between the farmer and the hind and there would be different deals done with each of the farm workers, depending on how useful the farmer felt each one to be.

Each farm worker was expected to supply some additional labour for the farm, usually his wife. The female labourer was given low skilled jobs to do, like hoeing and weeding turnips, or tying sheaves of wheat or barley. Where the hind had no wife or where the wife had small children, he was expected to employ a single woman, a bondager, to work on his behalf. Often the bondager would lodge with the hind and his family.

The farm workers lived in tied cottages on the farm. These were provided as part of the deal on pay, but when the job finished they had to get out of the house. On most farms the cottages were small, damp and overcrowded. They had no running water and few other facilities but, compared to conditions in the cities or in the miners rows, they were quite good.

Wage Rates
Another part of the pay agreement between the farmer and his farm workers was the right to a supply of fuel—coal, wood or peat—and a quantity of potatoes or other produce grown on the farm—for example, oats, barley or turnips. Most farm cottages also had a fairly generous garden in which to grow vegetables (in the Borders the tradition was that no farm worker planted his garden until after the May term, just in case he was not kept on at the farm). There was also space at the bottom of the garden to keep some livestock eg. hens or a pig, which could be fed from scraps from the house and on farm produce. These animals would, in turn, act as food for the farmworker's family. So, while agricultural wage rates were very low, there were some

35

Shearing and clipping sheep at Morar, Inverness-shire, 1910

perks to be found in working in agriculture and the standard of living was not as bad as it may at first appear.

Work Done in 1830

The work done on farms in 1830 was very hard indeed. The two main sources of energy were horse power and human power. Ploughing was done by horses, but it required the strength of a man to hold and steer the plough. Ploughing activities continued from the end of harvest until late Spring and were carried out whenever the ground was dry enough. Harrowing and preparing the ground for sowing was also done using horse power, but it required the ploughman to walk behind the

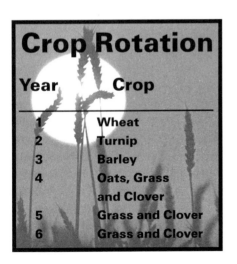

harrows to keep things right. The clearing of stones was a hard manual task and very often dykes or field boundaries were created from stones cleared in this way. Sowing the crop was usually done by hand and the seeds were then dug into the ground using harrows. Sometimes the field would be flattened by pulling a large stone roller over it. During the Spring months, cattle which had been wintered indoors were let out onto the grass parks and the manure which had built up in the sheds was cleared out and spread on the fields as fertiliser.

Once the crop was sown, life was fairly peaceful on an arable farm until early June when the harvest of hay for animal fodder began. This was dried then built into large stacks near the farm to feed horses and other livestock during the winter.

The crop was cut by hand using a sickle or a scythe. It was cut before it was quite ripe so that the valuable grains remained on the stalk. The womenfolk tied the wheat or barley stalks into armfuls or sheaves and then stood them in groups or stooks

to dry. These were then taken back to the farm to be built into stacks where they could be kept dry. In a reasonable year the harvest was finished by early October. Attention could then be turned to other crops. Potatoes had to be lifted using human power, the men digging and the women and children picking them up. Turnips had to be lifted and stored as animal feed for the winter. During the winter months the stacks of grain were taken bit by bit indoors to be threshed to separate the grain from the straw. The grain could then be used for a variety of purposes ranging from animal feed and whisky and beer making to milling it into meal for human consumption. Then the whole cycle started again. On most arable farms by 1830 there was a six year crop rotation system. Each field grew a different crop each year for six years and then it was returned to the crop grown in year one. The beauty of this system was that it provided hay and turnips for winter feed for livestock and the cereal crops for sale or for human consumption. Growing more grass meant that more animals could be kept over winter and therefore more manure would be produced to fertilise the cereal crops. Clover also draws nitrogen, a valuable nutrient, into the soil, so the land, while in permanent use, was not exhausted and was gaining plenty of nutrients.

Of course not all of Scotland was engaged in arable and livestock farming. This was mainly centred in Buchan, Angus, Fife, the Lothians, South East and South West Scotland. Other areas were simply not suitable for arable farming.

HILL FARMING

In some areas of Scotland, particularly in the North and West and in the Southern Uplands, the land was not suitable for arable purposes and was turned over to sheep. Large farm units of 1,000–2,000 acres were created. The tenant farmer would employ between 4 and 6 shepherds who would tend to a flock or hirsel of 500 sheep. This work required both great physical stamina and considerable skill. An average day's work might involve the ascent of two 3,000 foot mountains and a walk of more than 20 miles. The shepherd would also require many skills including dog handling and the ability to give emergency medical attention to the sheep.

Sheep Farming

Initially the main centre for sheep farming was in the hills of the Border area. After the failure of the 1745 rebellion and the destruction of the clan system, sheep were also introduced to the Highland areas. Although most of this took place before our period, there were still shepherds from the Borders walking huge flocks of Cheviot or Linton Blackface sheep north into newly created sheep farms as late as the 1860s. Since the skills of shepherding were quite unknown to the Highlanders, who were more used to working with cattle, most of the new shepherds were incomers. The surplus population, who had to leave the land to make way for the sheep farms was moved either to the shoreline or to the new industrial cities.

While these patterns of farming were widespread by 1830, they were by no means universal. All over Scotland there were also small tenant farms which had come into being for a number of reasons—sometimes accidentally. They were often developed as a way of improving very poor land. These farms were only big enough to support one man—sometimes not even big enough for that. Indeed, the tenant farmers would often work part-time for another farmer or for the estate. This, then, was the pattern of working, or employment, in agriculture in 1830. In many ways this pattern would not have changed greatly by 1930, though there were many pressures on it. Many of these seem at first sight to have little significance for Scottish Agriculture, but in fact they had a big impact.

Changing Patterns

The industrialisation which was occurring in Scotland at the time meant that there was an increased demand for food from the people living in the new industrial towns. This in itself created the need for changes in the way agriculture was organised in order to meet this demand. Transport links were not good enough at that time to gain adequate supplies from overseas. As a result, much new land was turned over to arable farming and there was a healthy demand for beef and mutton.

The textile industries were able to use the extra supplies of wool in their factories. At the same time, new developments in industry meant that new machinery and technology could be introduced to farms. Scots pioneers played an important part in this. Bell developed a reaping machine in 1828. New ploughs, which were not only lighter but also more efficient were developed. Also, new machinery for soil preparation, sowing and harvesting meant that the job could be done much more quickly and efficiently—and with less labour.

The old 'rigs' or ridges, which had been a feature of arable land in the farm towns, were flattened to allow the new machinery level ground on which to work. Even though the horse remained the main source of power for the bulk of the period, steam engines were used for other purposes. Mobile steam engines travelled around farms to help with the heavy work. Working in pairs, they could operate a plough by a system of chains. They could also work heavy lifting gear for stack building and for raising grain to lofts. Mobile threshing mills travelled round farms during the winter months, threshing and winnowing the grain, which saved on a great deal of hard work. Finally, the engine could work a bruising machine or even the mill wheels themselves. However, the steam engines were heavy and, therefore, not much use in the open field. The coming of the tractor,

An early binder harvesting barley near Biggar in the early 1900s

37

in the years after the First World War, signalled a change in agriculture that was to be as revolutionary as the agricultural revolution itself. The tractor was, in the space of the thirty years 1920–1950, to replace the horse as the main source of power. With its attachments and machines it would change the way virtually every job on the farm was done resulting in a whole new set of skills required for the farmworker—and, inevitably fewer jobs. By 1930 it was clear that the tractor and, indeed the combine harvester, were the tools of tomorrow and they were appearing on every go-ahead farm. However, they were for tomorrow. In 1930 fewer than 1 farm in 10 had a tractor and the first combine harvester had only made its appearance in Britain in 1926.

Golden Age of British Agriculture

Because food is such an important part of our life, agriculture, the food producer, has always enjoyed support from the government. In the 1830s and 1840s, Corn Laws prohibited the import of grain from overseas when the price of the home produce fell below a certain amount. This ensured that the farmers' income was kept at a reasonable level. On the other hand, it also meant that the price of bread and other foods which required flour was kept at an artificially high level. In fact, one result of this protection of agriculture was to make bread too expensive for agricultural workers. In 1846 the government decided to repeal the Corn Laws and allow free trade (ie. no import or export duties) for all goods. There was great fear that this would destroy British agriculture and put thousands out of work.

In fact, the years from 1850–1870 were called the Golden Age of British Agriculture. New inventions and discoveries meant that production from British farms increased steadily and could meet the demands of the rapidly growing population in the towns. At the same time the overseas producers were not able to compete. There were a series of good summers and bumper harvests. At this time, new, larger farmhouses were built, which in South East Scotland resembled small mansion houses. Also, new farm cottages and steadings were built. Sometimes the farm buildings were designed with towers and other decorations and remain today as minor architectural gems and monuments to prosperity. This prosperity was also invested in other improvements, like machinery and drainage. These new technologies reduced the demand for labour and between 1851 and 1871 the number of farm workers in Britain fell by 10%.

Depression

The Golden Age came to an abrupt end in the early 1870s.

There were a number of reasons for this. There was a succession of wet summers and bad harvests. Furthermore, disease spread among the cattle herds and sheep flocks. The new sheep farms which had been established on the hill areas began to suffer from the problems of overstocking. The amount of grass or nourishment available began to reduce because of overgrazing. Partly because of this, disease built up and spread rapidly through the flocks, causing huge losses.

Finally, technological advances meant that overseas producers could supply better quality crops far more cheaply than farmers could at home. In 1869 a railway line was completed in the USA which opened up the vast areas of the mid-west. Wheat grown there could be taken by train and steamship to Britain very easily. The development of the 'canning' process meant that meat could be put in tins in remote countries like Argentina and shipped to Britain to be

A Fordson tractor in Aberdeenshire in the 1920s

eaten. Thus corned beef became part of the British diet. The sheep stations in Australia could supply good quality wool for the textile industry and the development of refrigeration and freezing meant that butter and lamb could be brought from the farms of New Zealand halfway round the world and be sold to the British housewife more cheaply than home produce.

British agriculture faced disaster. Prices fell, farmers went out of business and the number of agricultural workers dropped steadily. British farmers were forced to concentrate on production of items which could not easily be imported, like milk and vegetables. Livestock production concentrated on quality rather than quantity. Scottish farms developed beef breeds like the Aberdeen Angus and Galloway, which were world leaders in their time, and this livestock was exported to establish and improve the herds overseas. The effect of these developments on farm workers was very significant as wages were kept low and there was a steady drift away from work in agriculture. At the same time, the fall in profits in agriculture meant that there was a fall in the rents charged and a fall in income for the large estates. In Highland Scotland, some estates gave up on sheep altogether and turned the land over to deer forest, which could be used for sport and could be rented out to others. It was at this time that shooting lodges were built all over the Highlands to meet this need. However, this could not be called agriculture and although it provided jobs for ghillies and stalkers, it contributed to further depopulation of the rural areas.

Even tenant farmers had problems. If they fell into debt they faced eviction from their farms

Women workers at the harvest during World War I on Orkney. (Note the soldier home on leave)

by their landlord. The government tried to help them by passing laws in 1875, 1906 and 1908 which gave them some security on their farms. With this security they were encouraged to invest in improvements to their land. However, by the start of the twentieth century the government considered it more important to provide cheap food for the population of Britain's industrial towns than to preserve our own agriculture industry as a major food producer.

By 1914 Britain imported nearly 60% of all her foodstuffs.

Crofting

One positive development to come out of this period was the improvement in the way of life of the remaining smallholders in the Highlands who had suffered very badly at the hands of the landowners. They were often seen as a nuisance and were pushed out by any means possible to make way for sheep farms or deer forest. Rents had risen steadily during the depression and in 1882 a period of civil disobedience called the Crofters War began throughout the Highland area (See pages 14—16). Troops were called in to put down the disturbances. In 1884 the government appointed a Royal Commission, the Napier Commission, to look into the problems of poverty and landholding in the Highlands.

The evidence given to the Commission paints a dreadful picture of poverty and oppression. In 1886 the government passed a Crofters Act which gave the crofters security of tenure as long as the rent was paid and which also established a Commission to determine fair rents and to cancel rent arrears. Inevitably, this created a demand for more crofts and in the late 1880s there were land raids in a number of areas. Poor cottars with no crofts of their own staked claims to land which was suitable for crofts, but which was only being used for sheep or deer farming.

These land raiders were punished by the law, but gradually more land was made available.

The First World War

The outbreak of the First World War soon revealed the dangers of importing so much food. German submarines, waiting off the west coast of Britain, could sink merchant ships bringing supplies and raw materials to Britain and very nearly succeeded. In 1916 and 1917 the Germans tried to starve Britain into surrender by stopping food supplies getting in. The government encouraged the production of home grown food again.

The Corn Production Act of 1917 guaranteed a minimum price for corn to encourage

Building a stack of hay in East Lothian in the 1920s

farmers to grow as much as possible. Subsidies were offered to increase the amount of land cultivated. Land which had not been used for arable purposes since the Golden Age some fifty years before was ploughed up, and sheep and cattle were again established on the hills from which they had been cleared to make way for deer. A minimum wage for agricultural workers was laid down to encourage them to stay on the land. Farming was a reserved occupation and it was possible to claim exemption from Military Service if you were engaged in essential farm work. However, many farm workers joined the army and their places were taken by women. Often these women were not from farms themselves and the members of the Land Army were nicknamed the Lilac and Sunbonnet Brigade. They coped well with the demands of farm work, particularly since the introduction of machinery had reduced the amount of heavy manual work. The Land Army, at its height, was over 16,000 strong and it made a valuable contribution to the War effort.

From the end of the War in 1918 until 1930, British agriculture went through another signifi-

cant period of depression. Government subsidies were removed and the Corn Production Act was repealed. Once again cheap foreign food flooded into Britain and the British farmers could not compete. Farm incomes fell and many farmers went out of business. This was particularly hard on the ex-servicemen who had taken advantage of the promise of 'land fit for heroes' and had taken up tenancies on smallholdings specially created for them in the arable areas. In the crofting counties ex-servicemen demanded land for crofts from their landlords and in the Western Isles there were 'land raids' again where men pegged out claims of land for their crofts. Even though these men were initially charged with lawbreaking and some were even put in prison, additional areas for crofting were created and in some areas, notably Vatersay, the Department of Agriculture actually bought an estate which it turned over for crofting purposes. For all these groups the 1920s were hungry years.

There was bitterness among the farm workers, as farmers tried to abandon the minimum wage principle. This provoked a strike, almost unheard of in agriculture, in 1923. The result of this was the concession of a minimum wage of £1.5/- per week for a 50 hour week and a half day holiday each week. By 1930 agriculture was still a hard way to earn a living.

LIVING AND WORKING CONDITIONS
As an industry, agriculture was unique. Unlike the factories or coal mines where hundreds might be employed and the boss could be a remote almost unknown figure, the farm was a relatively small work unit, employing no about 12 people, all

of whom the farmer would know personally. This may perhaps explain why trade unionism in agriculture was never as powerful or successful as it was in other industries.

Trade Unions
The most famous trade unionists of all, The Tolpuddle Martyrs, were agricultural labourers. In 1834 six men tried to establish a union branch at Tolpuddle in Dorset. It was decided to make an example of them. They were found guilty of swearing a secret oath when joining the union and were sentenced to be transported to Australia for seven years.

It was not until 1872 that the National Agricultural Labourers Union was formed by Joseph Arch. Initially this was very successful, organising strikes and managing to raise pay rates by up to 50% in some areas. At its peak in 1874 it had 86,000 members, but the agricultural depression which followed had a bad effect on the Union and by 1889 it had only 5,000 members. In Scotland there was a long tradition of ploughman's or whipman's societies. These were not so much unions as friendly societies which helped sick members. In the 1800s localised unions were established and ran for a time demanding, amongst other things, basic wages of fifteen shillings per week, a ten hour working day in summer and an eight hour day in winter. Although they achieved some successes, these local unions faded out after a time. It was not until 1912 that a Scottish Farm Servants Union was formed. It was a national union and campaigned for all farm workers in Scotland, seeking longer engagements than six month terms, monthly payment rather than six monthly and one half day holiday per week. By 1930 agricul-

Farm workers in a bothy on a farm in Angus

farmer's wife or else by the maid or 'Kitchie deem'. Bothy life has been much romanticised. It was basic, tough and not very healthy. During the winter nights the men of the bothy would amuse themselves by playing melodions or mouth organs and singing songs, some of which were locally composed. These bothy ballads were often earthy and were satirical about the farms and the grieve (farm manager).

At certain times during the year, parties or 'Kirns' would be held on the farm. The grain loft, with a well-sprung wooden floor, would be cleared and decorated and a dance held. Often the music and entertainment was provided by the farm hands.

Migrant Labour

At busy times during the farming year, particularly at harvest time, additional labour would be recruited onto the farms. In the early 1830s there were often migrants from the Highland areas, frequently women, who would come to the farms to cut and bind the wheat and barley. After the Irish famines in the 1840s they were largely replaced by Irish migrants who came over for the season. These people would come over early in April to plant the potatoes, would travel from farm to farm doing the jobs as they came up—weeding, shearing, thinning, harvest-

tural trade unions were still not powerful and lacked a strong sense of national unity.

On each farm however, the men employed could find their own ways of improving their conditions. Using humour, supersitition and other forms of gentle suggestion, they could persuade the farmer and his wife to improve conditions. Furthermore, any farm which was noted for the harsh methods of the farmer, poor pay or the poor food supplied by the farmer's wife was liable to find it hard to attract suitable labour. Farm workers may well not have enjoyed good pay and conditions but neither did they live in terror or servility.

Accommodation

In 1830 living conditions on farms could be fairly basic. Most 'cottars', or workers, houses were single roomed, approximately 4 metres square. The walls were less than two metres high, the roof was thatched and there was no ceiling. The room was divided inside by wooden box beds and the floor was of clay or trampled earth. They were in rows of four or more, close to the farm and steading.

During the 1800s there was a process of rebuilding which peaked during the Golden Age between 1850 and 1870. The workers' homes were built in rows of anything from four to twelve houses. These were of the 'but and ben' variety, sometimes with a second storey added. The floors were stone or wood and the roofs were slate. These houses were still in use in 1930 and can be seen, much improved and extended, today. Running water and toilets were being introduced but were not widespread before 1930. Whole families might work on the farm at busy times and taking a single farm worker as a lodger was not uncommon. This could be a single woman bondager or a young man. Other single men stayed in the bothy or chaumer. These buildings were usually part of the farm steading. They were very basic buildings, having a fire, built-in wooden beds, with chaff filled mattresses, and kists, or chests, for the belongings of the men who lived there. The main difference between a bothy and a chaumer was that in the bothy the occupants cooked for themselves, while those in the chaumer were fed in the farm kitchen either by the

Numbers Employed in Agriculture in Scotland	
Year	No. Employed
1831	800,000
1881	269,000
1901	210,000
1931	178,000

Table 3.1   Source: Various

A Fife ploughman with his pair o' horse in the 1920s

ing—and finally, after lifting and storing the potato crop in October, they would return to Ireland for the winter months. They stayed in even more basic bothies on the farms they visited. The theory was that since they were migrants they would not look after any decent furniture that they were given.

FARMING AND FARM WORK IN 1930

How, then, had employment and working conditions on the land changed in the years between 1830 and 1930? If you compare farming with other industries, the short answer would appear to be 'remarkably little'. The pay of agricultural workers still lagged behind that of workers in other industries. Agricultural work was often regarded as being unskilled, even though the work carried out with livestock, crops and machinery required a great deal of skill. However, the coming of a statutory (backed by the law) minimum wage was certainly of great benefit to the workers. The nature of the work done on the farms was still similar to that done in 1830. Despite the fact that technology had pro-

vided machinery for a whole range of farm jobs, there was still a great deal of hard physical labour to be done.

Horse power continued to be the dominant work tool and as long as that remained, the working day of the ploughman would still be long and hard. His day would start as early as 4.00 am with feeding the horses and end at about 9.00pm with a final look at the horses to see them bedded down. There were fewer people employed in agriculture as mechanisation saved jobs and as the depressions forced the farmers to economise and have fewer people in the 'farm town'. (See Ttable 3.1.) As a consequence the social life declined and villages became more attractive

places than individual farms for workers to live. The housing conditions improved slowly but steadily over the period and, though far from perfect, the living conditions were certainly better than the slums of the industrial cities. In the Highlands, the crofts provided a stable and secure way of life, even though by 1930 most of them were not big enough to provide a decent living for a family. As for the big estates and the great landowners, their heyday was past. Levels of wealth and prosperity were never the same after the First World War. Death Duties, a tax imposed by the Liberal Government in 1909, had a crippling effect on some estates and led to large areas of land being sold off. This led, in some places, to the emergence of a farmer who was the owner of his farm rather than a tenant.

The agricultural way of life continued to operate in relatively small units. The size of farms tended to increase gradually in order to make economies of scale. However, the number of men employed in each unit did not increase. This fragmentation seriously hindered the development of a national trade union.

It is probably fair to say, when describing changes in agriculture between 1830 and 1930, that more things stayed the same than changed.

A travelling threshing mill in Lauderdale (Note the steam engine in the background)

EVALUATION EXERCISE

living and working on the land

The following activities refer to the information given in Sources A—H.

Source A

This is an extract from the *New Statistical Account,* a survey of all Scottish Parishes which was written in 1839. It concerns the parish of Luss in Dumbartonshire.

The ordinary labour of cultivation is generally performed by the farmer's own family and servants, who live at his house, and are hired half yearly. The average hire for a full grown man is £7.00 and a woman, £3.10/- (£3.50) per half year. Persons hired for harvest labour receive, men 2/- (10p) and women 1/6 (8p) per day with victuals. Occasional labourers receive 2/- (10p) per day.

Source B

This is an extract from the *Third Statistical Account*. It is also about Luss and was written in 1952.

Not many local people are employed on the farms, which are mostly tended by the families; moreover, machinery has made it unnecessary to employ many people.

Source C

This source is taken from *The Standard Cyclopedia of Modern Agriculture* which was published in 1909. This extract describes bothies.

This is the name given to a system of housing unmarried male servants ... This is usually a large single apartment building standing by itself or abutting on to the steading with bed cubicles around for the occupants to sleep in. Not so long ago it was the custom to provide the bothy men with sleeping accommodation over the stables or in some similar convenient place, but since the requirements of the sanitary authorities became more exacting, it has been found necessary to do away with much of this class of bedroom accommodation and provide something better. Even yet it cannot be said that the sleeping accommodation provided on most farms for the bothy men is luxurious, although as a rule it is quite healthy and comfortable.

Whatever may be said against the bothy from a social and moral point of view—and few would care to defend it in either respect—there is no doubt that it has compensating advantages. In no other way would it be possible for young men engaged in farm labour to live so cheaply. So long as they are content with the natural food products which come their way as part of the price of their labour, they have practically no expenditure.

Questions

1. What changes in agricultural employment are identifed in sources A and B?

2. How useful are these sources for learning about employment in agriculture in Scotland?

3. Explain the positive and negative aspects of the bothy system described in Source C.

4. Study Source D. Account for the changes shown on the graph.

Source D

This graph is printed in Sauvain, *BritishSocial & Economic History*.

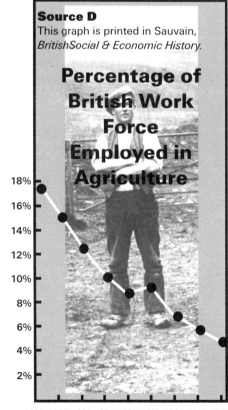

Percentage of British Work Force Employed in Agriculture

18%
16%
14%
12%
10%
8%
6%
4%
2%

1861 1871 1881 1891 1901 1911 1921 1931 1941

Killin
11th December 1880

Dear James,

Referring to our conversation when I was in Morvern and our correspondence since, I cannot see any way at all to enter into a lease of the farms at the present rent. As you are aware, I considered the rent much too high when you entered into the new arrangement with Mr Newton about two years ago and _most reluctantly_ then I yielded. _Since then_ a great change has taken place in the value of farms the fall in rent all round being from 10 to 40 per cent.

The Season now past is no doubt an improvement on the former one as far as the price of stock is concerned. But then wool the best item you have altogether is all but unsaleable.

I am quite sure that Mr Newton has no wish to exact from you more than the place is worth. I consider £500 the _outside_ value of it including the improvements and at this it is dear. I am quite willing to make a trial of it at this rent if Mr Newton can see his way to reduce it so far.

But times are so exceedingly precarious and uncertain that even at this I would not be willing to enter into a lease without a break at the end of two years. Why if the prospect of importing fresh meat from Australia is successful there will be an end to Scottish sheep farming. I am told too that the import of long coarse wool such as Highland wool from South America is increasing year by year.

I am
Your affectionate Brother
R. A. Robertson.

Source E
This source is a letter written by Robert Robertson, a banker in Killin, Perthshire, to his brother James, a tenant farmer in Morvern, Argyllshire.

Question

1 What problems for tenant farmers in the 1880s are highlighted by these letters?

Killin
3rd June 1885

Dear Mr Newton,

Seeing you have agreed to reduce the rent of Kinloch and Rahoy, Morvern occupied by my brothers, to £450 per annum I hereby guarantee payment of the rent thereof to you for the next four years, from Whitsunday 1885.

Yours faithfully,
R. A. Robertson

Source F
This source is a letter written by Robert Robertson to Mr Newton, his brother's landlord in Morvern.

Source G

This source comes from a book entitled *An Auld Herd's Memories*, published in 1983. It was written by a shepherd called Walter Ramage. Here he describes his life in the early 1920s.

It was coming on for the end of November again and that was settling up time. The rest of the herds were all flitting except the Phaup one so when he came to me I said I wanted a regular ewe hirsel as I was fed up with the droving. He said he would give me one in at Hindhope but I did not fancy that as he was not an easy man to get on with and we had not had any troubles so far so I wanted to keep it that way. About a week after that I got a letter from the Head Herd at Calroust who I had marched with at Mainside, saying he wanted a young man to herd the West Side and he would like to meet me at the Pub at Hownam on the Friday night and if I could not get down I was to come over on the Sunday. I did not get the letter till the Saturday morning as the Plenderleith herd brought the mail out with him so I went over to see them on the Sunday. We had our tea and then had a walk up the burn a bit and Peter said he had heard that I wanted a change. He said if it hadna been Sunday what wage was I wanting to herd the West Side. I said if it hadna been Sunday I would want and stated my sum. 'Well Wat', he says, 'if it hadna been Sunday I would just gie that', so 'well', say I, 'that's settled' and I was fixed up again and landed in the Bowmont Water the following year. I stayed two years when the Place was sold and the new man had his own herds coming so did not need us.

Source H

These cartoons are taken from *Punch* magazine. The cartoon on the left appeared in 1915 and the cartoon on the right in 1917.

FARMER. (who has got lady-help in the dairy). " 'ULLO MISSY, WHAT IN THE WORLD BE YOU DOIN'?"
LADY. "WELL, YOU TOLD ME TO WATER THE COWS AND I'M DOING IT. THEY DON'T SEEM TO LIKE IT MUCH."

WOMAN-POWER

CERES. "SPEED THE PLOUGH."
PLOUGHMAN. "I DON'T KNOW WHO YOU ARE MA'AM, BUT IT'S NO GOOD SPEEDING THE PLOUGH UNLESS WE CAN GET THE WOMEN TO DO THE HARVESTING."
[Fifty thousand more women are wanted on the land to take the place of men called to the colours, if the harvest is to be got in.]

Questions

1 What changing attitudes to women's work in agriculture are identifed in these sources?

2 How useful are these sources for identifying changing attitudes?

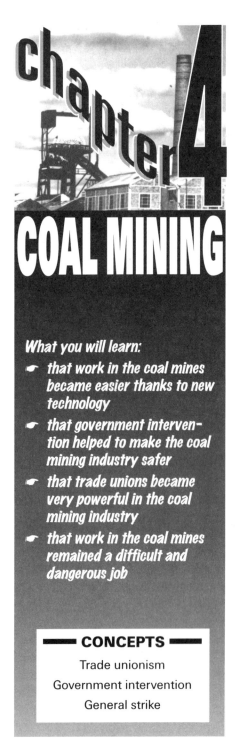

chapter 4
COAL MINING

What you will learn:

- ☞ that work in the coal mines became easier thanks to new technology
- ☞ that government intervention helped to make the coal mining industry safer
- ☞ that trade unions became very powerful in the coal mining industry
- ☞ that work in the coal mines remained a difficult and dangerous job

═══ CONCEPTS ═══

Trade unionism

Government intervention

General strike

COAL MINING was always difficult, dangerous and physically demanding work which many people were unwilling to take on. Up to the end of the eighteenth century Scottish miners were forced to work in a mine for life. They could not leave when they wanted to and any who ran away could be hunted down, brought back to the mine and punished. Miners were also expected to bind their families to the pit. Laws were only passed to stop this 'slavery' in 1775. In this way a steady supply of labour was generated, which was just as well since there was not a ready supply of people wanting to work in the mines. Miners were not popular generally, and since the mines were often located in fairly remote areas they were truly a race apart. Because of the isolation, the miners tended to live together in pit villages which were located close to the pit shafts. Conditions in these villages were primitive and unattractive and they were not often visited by outsiders.

WORK IN THE MINES IN 1830

The mines were usually owned by the local landowner and were run by a grieve or manager. This man may not have known a great deal about the techniques of mining, but he had great power. He paid the miners, ensured that there was a work force, organised the pit housing and collected rents. He oversaw the selling of the coal and acted as judge and jury to any misbehaviour on the part of the miners or their families. Clearly, he had great power over them.

In the pit, the man in charge was the oversman, who was knowledgeable about mining techniques. Under him was the checksman, whose job it was to count and check the amount of coal brought to the surface by each miner. Since miners were paid on piece work, ie. by the amount of coal produced, this was a very responsible job and there were many arguments between the checksman and the miners about the precise amounts of coal measured.

As the industrial revolution in coal mining intensified, many mine owners gave up trying to run their pits and leased them instead to industrialists who had money to invest in the new steam engines and other machinery needed for deeper pits. They in turn appointed professional managers to run the pits. The work force, however, tended to come from the same groups, with new workers being taken from the immigrant people drawn to the industrial centres from the countryside and from Ireland. Pay rates for miners in the early 1830s were relatively good—somewhere in the region of 5/- (25p) a day. This was much more than in many other industries and was designed to attract workers. It was generally unsuccessful.

Hewers

The work down the mines was organised on a team basis, the team often being a family. The leader of the team, the man of the family, was the hewer, the person who cut the coal from the face. Depending on the seam, he either stood at the face or crouched, or sometimes even

A hewer at work

lay on his side to break the coal away from the face. The work was skilled and dangerous. The more coal cut the more money earned. However, it was important to break it off in large lumps since they were more valuable. While it was important to work quickly, it was equally important to take care, since careless work could cause accidents—even a roof fall.

Conditions at the face were extremely dusty and lung disease was very common. As the mines became deeper, so the dangers of gas increased along with the problems associated with a lack of ventilation. Deeper shafts and coalfaces further from the surface lead to hot conditions and it was not unusual for the hewer to work with few, if indeed any, clothes on.

Bearers

The other members of the team were the bearers. Their job was to move the cut coal from the coalface to the bottom of the shaft and then up to the surface. Very often it was the job of the children to shift the coal about the seams. This they did in a variety of ways. Most either carried the coal on their backs in creels or dragged it in sledges along the rough surface of the mine floor. In some of the advanced pits, wooden wagonways—rough rails—had been laid so that wheeled trucks could be pulled or pushed along the tracks by the bearers. In this way the heavier loads could be shifted. This work was suited to children as, being smaller in stature, they could work more easily in areas with low roofs.

Once at the base of the shaft, the coal had to be carried to the surface. In some mines in 1830 it was still the task of women to carry the coal in baskets on their backs up the sets of ladders to

Bearer carrying coal to the surface.

the surface. However, as mines became deeper this work was much more commonly done by lifts and pulleys, operated by either a horse gin or a water wheel. Only when the coal reached the surface was it tallied to find out the amount produced by each team and this determined the rate of pay. There were many arguments at this stage, since it was in the interests of the checksman to make sure that he did not pay out for poor quality material—ie. too many stones or insufficiently filled baskets, while the miner and his team wanted to ensure that they were not cheated in any way out of the stuff they had produced.

The amount produced by each

team varied, depending on the mood of the hewer, the quality of the face he was working on and the amount of time wasted. In general the teams were expected to work for 6 days per week, 12 hours per day, but this was not always the case. Since there was such a shortage of labour, the hewers did not live in fear and terror of the boss—they were unlikely to be sacked. Because they were also relatively well paid they were not afraid to take a few days off work. They would spend their time socialising and drinking, much to the annoyance of their supervisors and bosses.

Trappers

In the newer pits another job, that of trapper, had emerged for younger children. To ensure a through flow of ventilation, it was necessary to close off certain passages to ensure that the air travelled throughout the pit. This was done by a series of trap doors. However, these doors had to be opened and closed to allow the bearers to pass with their loads. This job was entrusted to the children too young and/or weak to act as bearers. A twelve hour shift in a dark dusty coal mine with little company could hardly be described as a pleasant experience for a young child. On the other hand it did release the parents from looking after them and this enabled both parents to work. The trappers could often look after even younger children in the family at the same time.

GOVERNMENT REFORMS

The 1830s was a period of great reform. The government began to move away from its policies of 'laissez faire', which means they let people do exactly what they wanted, and began to pass laws concerning the fair treatment of working people.

In 1833 an Act of Parliament was passed, limiting the hours a child could be made to work in a factory, and in the 1840s it was the turn of the coal mines. In 1840 a Royal Commission on children's employment was established. It published a Blue Book in 1842 on conditions for underground workers. The report described appalling work practices, quoting accounts from people who worked in the mines and describing the work they had to do. This painted a very bleak picture indeed.

Children and women were used as beasts of burden and had to work in dangerous and unpleasant conditions. The report

quoted eyewitness accounts which were undoubtedly accurate. However, the report did not give anything like an exact picture of working conditions in British coal mines.

In many of the newer mines, the heavy dragging and lifting had been made much easier by using simple machinery or even horse power. It is estimated that there were about 150,000 people working in the coal mines in 1840, of whom only about 6,000 were women. The team system was already old-fashioned when it was described in 1840. Why, then, was the report so full of accounts of hardship? There is little doubt that the authors of the report wanted to draw attention to the harsh conditions for women and children in mines and therefore highlighted them. After all, who would bother to read a report that described a boring, safe and predictable job?

The 1830s and '40s was a time when the social conscience of Victorian Britain was being stirred by the work of Edwin Chadwick with the Poor Law, William Wilberforce with the anti-slavery movement, Elizabeth Fry with prison reform and Lord Ashley (later Earl of Shaftesbury) with factory and

mine reform. The work of Charles Dickens also contributed to these feelings. *Oliver Twist*, for example, embarrassed middle-class Britain.

Mines Act 1842

As a direct result of the Royal Commission Report, the Mines Act of 1842 was passed. This banned women and girls and boys under the age of 10 from work underground. Both women and children could continue to work in the coal industry in the many dirty and difficult jobs above ground, for example, sorting and bagging the coal. The minimum age for operating a winding engine to work in the shafts was set at 15.

To enforce the Act the government appointed one inspector for the whole of Britain. He was not given the right to go down pits until 1850. Needless to say, many pits ignored the new law and kept on using children whenever they could reasonably do so. Since compulsory registration of births only began in 1855, it was difficult to prove the age of a child anyway. The miners' families were keen to keep their children working, since they produced valuable extra income for the family. However, the principle of the government

A trapper at work, circa 1840.

Carrying coal up the shaft

appointing an inspector was accepted.

The work done by women underground, the heavy dragging and lifting, was being phased out anyway and it is fair to say that technological advance, rather than government legislation, forced women to stop working underground.

Although it was a very positive step to stop women and children working underground, it did undoubtedly cause problems for the mining families. The coal mines tended to be isolated in areas where there was no other ready source of employment. Unless the women could find above ground work at the pit, they were likely to be put out of work. One Scottish study discovered that of 2,400 women thrown out of work in the mines in 1842, only 200 had managed to find other work by 1845. The other negative aspect of the Mines Act of 1842 was that it completely ignored the working conditions of men and boys over the age of 10. There was nothing done at all to deal with the very real problems of safety, working conditions and the length of working day. That was still to come in the future.

It would not be fair to be too negative about the 1842 Mines Act. Despite the fact that it was very limited in scope, it was at least a start, and it began the practice of government action and legislation in the coal mines and other industries, which was to result in great improvements to working conditions over the next century.

Other Government Reforms

In 1850 an Act for the Inspection of Coal Mines appointed more inspectors and gave them the right to go underground. They were also given powers to collect information about accidents and it became a legal requirement to report all fatal accidents to the Home Office. In this way it became possible to collect information about accidents and their causes. The inspectors were also given powers to enforce rules and regulations about safety in mines and to prosecute anyone they found breaking them. In the early stages there were very few prosecutions, but the principle was a very valuable one to establish. Finally, the Act made it necessary to prepare and register a plan of the mine workings.

In 1855, an additional Act required each colliery to draw up its own safety rules and to have them approved by the Home Office. There were further Acts in 1860 and 1862 which introduced safety rules in line with the advances in technology being made at that time. The 1862 Act, for example, made it compulsory for each mine to have at least two exits. This not only improved ventilation, it also provided a safe exit for the miners in the case of an accident in one of the shafts. The 1860 Act forbade boys under 12 from going underground unless they could read and write.

In 1872 it was made compulsory for the mine manager to hold a certificate of competency which was only gained after passing a national exam. At the same time, the Act gave the mine workers the right to appoint their own safety representative to inspect their mine.

In 1909 an eight hour working day was introduced for underground workers and in 1911 the Coal Mines Bill required larger collieries to provide baths at the pit head. In 1917 another hour was taken off the working day, reducing it to seven hours.

Dangers

Despite these improvements the mines remained dangerous places. As they got deeper, longer and larger, so the risks of roof falls, explosions and flooding increased. Accidents were an everyday occurrence. In some ways the new technology caused even more risks, as the early versions of equipment and machinery were often dangerous and unreliable.

Fatal accidents were not uncommon. By far the worst occurred at High Blantyre in 1877, when 200 men were killed. The reason for the disaster was an explosion, caused by a naked light. In 1894 four men were killed when a winding rope broke in their shaft and the lift fell to the bottom. In 1909 ten men were killed in Ayrshire when old mine workings collapsed in on them, causing flooding.

Production

During the century there was a phenomenal growth in the coal mining industry. This was due to the increased demand for coal and the technological advances which made it possible for more coal to be produced. New pits were opened and new areas were developed. This in turn created a need for more men to work in the pits. The numbers employed in the British coal industry rose from 250,000 in 1830 to 500,000 in 1880. Numbers employed reached a peak of 1,100,000 in 1910, before slipping back to 780,000 in 1930. At the same time the amount of coal produced in Britain rose from 30 million tons per year to 150 million tons in 1880, peaked at 270 million tons in 1910 and dropped back to 220 million tons in 1930. During this time coal became Scotland's largest industry, employing the most people.

New Workers

A ready supply of new workers for the mines came from the large numbers of migrant and immigrant workers who were drawn to central Scotland at that time. The clearances and the movement of population from rural Scotland owing to the changes in agriculture meant that there was a surplus of men looking for work. After the 1840s there was also a huge influx of poor immigrants from Ireland. This included both Ulster Protestants and Roman Catholics from Southern Ireland. Religious friction between these communities was not uncommon and steps were taken to deal with this. In east Dumbartonshire for instance, new villages were built for new mine workings. One village, Croy, was for Roman Catholics whilst another, Twechar, was for Protestants. Whole new towns grew up around the coal mining areas. Coatbridge, for instance, grew from a population of 2,000 in 1831 to 22,000 in 1871. The historians Sydney and Olive Checkland say of it, "It was a place of dreadful overcrowding, filth, disease, drunkenness, violence and prostitution, a kind of frontier town in which civil society scarcely existed".

The Scottish and Irish elements were almost equally balanced. In 1861, 44% of Coatbridge colliers were Irish. In the years after the First World War new immigrant groups from Eastern and Southern Europe began to settle in the mining areas and they too found work in the coal mines.

TRADE UNIONS

The men who worked in the coal mines held a strong common identity, therefore it is not surprising that trade unions took a powerful hold in the coal industry from a fairly early time. Reasons can be found for this in that life in a coal mining community, often in a fairly isolated area, drew people together. In addition to this, the power of the bosses in the coal mines was exceptional. Not only did they control who got jobs, they also determined the level of wages, owned the miners' houses and controlled their spending, since they often owned the local shop. In some areas the miners were not paid in money but in tokens, which could only be spent in the company shop. This was known as the truck system.

Faced with this power, any individual who wanted to complain stood little chance. Only if the community acted together could anything be gained. In the early years there were disagreements and strikes but, lacking organisation, these were easily defeated. Even the law officers could be relied upon to side with the bosses.

The first attempt to form a 'union' came with the formation of the Miners Association of Great Britain in 1841. This was based in Wakefield in Yorkshire, but transferred to Scotland. It organised a number of strikes during the 1840s, aimed at improving pay and conditions, but it had little success and had collapsed by 1848. In 1855 Alexander MacDonald, a miner who had worked hard to gain a university education, was the first secretary of the United Coal and Iron Mines Association. After a successful strike by Lanarkshire miners, he persuaded other areas to join the Association. He argued that miners needed a centralised, national union to be powerful enough to take on the bosses.

In 1870, the success of the Fife and Kinross miners in forcing an 8 hour working day persuaded others that similar organisations should be founded and in 1873 a Scottish Federation was established. In 1874 MacDonald was elected to Parliament for North Staffordshire and spoke up for the miners there. He managed to gain improvements in safety and ventilation and obtained a shorter working day. In addition

Numbers Employed in Coal Mining in Scotland

Year	Numbers
1854	33,000
1881	181,000
1901	112,000
1931	121,000

Table 4.1
Source: Various

he oversaw the introduction of check weighers who accurately tallied the amount of coal mined so that the miners could be paid fairly.

The next great leader was Keir Hardie, a man who had begun working in the Lanarkshire mines at the age of 11. In 1880 he was the leader of the Ayrshire Miners. He began a campaign for recognition of the miners' unions by the owners—initially unsuccessfully. He too believed that the miners needed to be centrally organised and in 1894 the Scottish Miners Federation affiliated to the Miners Federation of Great Britain. There was a huge strike in 1894 and even though this strike did not achieve its aims, the publicity encouraged more miners to join the union. Keir Hardie also became an MP, the first for the newly formed Labour Party in 1892. Robert Smillie was his successor as leader of the miners.

Twentieth Century

Towards the start of the twentieth century the main concern of the unions, and the miners, was to break away from the tradition of a sliding scale for pay. Put simply, this related miners' pay to the price of coal. The higher the price of coal the higher the wage paid. Since it required the same amount of work to produce the coal regardless of its selling price, this was clearly unfair.

In 1894 a Conciliation Board agreed that a minimum wage for miners should be set. They took the average wage for a miner in 1888 (roughly 4 shillings, or 20p per day) as the basis to work on. The minimum wage for 1900 was set at 31.25% above the 1888 level (roughly 5 shillings and threepence, or 26p). They also set a maximum pay rate of 75% above the 1888 level (roughly 7

shillings or 35p). This principle remained in force for many years, though the coal owners did try to reduce the minimum wage when coal prices began to fall heavily. The minimum level was raised to 50% above the 1888 level (6 shillings or 30p) a few years later, when it was discovered that this was the level set in England.

Wages above the minimum however, still depended on a sliding scale. When the miners went on strike there were inevitable knock-on effects on the rest of British industry and many other workers were laid off. In 1912, after the longest strike ever seen in Britain and lasting 12 weeks, the minimum wage for all miners was agreed and confirmed by law when the Miners Minimum Wage Act was passed. Membership of the Scottish Miners Union continued to increase steadily from 50,000 members in 1900 to 87,000 in 1913.

The power of one or two industries over the rest of Britain was not lost on the Unions and in 1914 the Triple Industrial Alliance was agreed. This was a promise by the three most powerful Unions to support each other in industrial disputes. The Unions were the Miners Federation, the National Union of Railwaymen and the National Transport Workers Federation. These three, acting together, could paralyse Britain. The outbreak of the First World War delayed the plans for action.

The First World War

With the outbreak of the First World War in 1914 the coal mines were taken under the control of the government. This was to make sure that this essential industry produced as much coal as possible to support the war effort. Coal miners were considered so important that

they were exempt from war service. This was a relatively good period for the miners as government control resulted in increased safety standards, higher wages and the same wage paid in all areas. Pay deals were negotiated between management and workers and, overall, there was very little unrest. Miners were generally happy to have the mines run by the government and would have been pleased for this to continue on a permanent basis by having the mines nationalised (owned by the government).

The War, however, brought problems as well as benefits for the coal industry. Before the War Britain had exported more than 60 million tons of coal annually overseas but this stopped completely during the War and never returned to this level after it. Furthermore, the technological advances which were stimulated by the War, eg. oil fired engines and electricity, were, in the future, to reduce significantly the demand for coal at home. After the War finished in 1918, there was a debate about who should own the mines and the government appointed a Royal Commission to look into it. When the Sankey Commission reported in 1919 it recommended that the coal mines should stay under government control. However, the Prime Minister, Lloyd George, was put under great pressure by the owners to give the coal mines back to them. When he did this the miners were very angry because he had promised to follow the advice of the Royal Commission.

General Strike

When the mines were handed back to their owners in 1921 the coal industry was going through a very bad time. The boom in industry as people replaced things after the War was short lived and the price of coal, which had reached £4.00 per ton, had fallen to £1.75 per ton. This was because there was a fall in demand from overseas markets and also at home. The mine owners let it be known that when they took control of the mines again they would cut wages to make sure that the industry continued to remain profitable. Furthermore, the common pay levels throughout the country would be replaced by regional agreements, since some areas were more profitable than others.

The Scottish coalfield, overall, was one of the least profitable and could therefore expect the lowest pay rates. Even in the prosperous year of 1920 the Scottish coalfield made an overall loss of £5 million.

The Miners Federation, which was unhappy about the mines being returned to the owners, was even more unhappy about the proposed wage cuts. The miners refused to accept the owners' terms and called a strike for 15 April 1921. They also asked their allies in the Triple Alliance to support them. However, on the day the other two Unions backed out and left the miners to fight on alone. This was a bad day for the miners and was called 'Black Friday'. The miners stayed on strike for nearly three months, but eventually had to go back to work on the terms offered by the owners.

There was a further fall in coal prices in 1925, this time to below £1.00 per ton. The mine owners again proposed to cut wages and to extend the length of the working day by one hour. The Miners Union refused to accept this and used the slogan 'not a penny off the pay, not a second on the day' to gain public support. This time the Triple Alliance supported them. The government avoided the crisis by giving a subsidy of £24 million to make up for the owners' wage cuts. This great victory for the Trade Unions was hailed as 'Red Friday', but the success was short-lived. The subsidy was only to last for 9 months and nothing was resolved during this time.

When the subsidy ended on 1 May 1926, the Trades Union Congress called a General Strike to begin on Tuesday 4 May 1926. Many people feared that the aim of the strike was the destruction of the British way of life, but in actual fact it was aimed at supporting the miners who were facing what were seen as unreasonable demands from their employers. The General Strike only lasted for nine days before the TUC called it off, but the miners stayed on strike for six months before going back to work on the terms demanded by the employers. The strike had a devastating effect on the coal industry. Many of the smaller pits were forced to close down because of the loss of money; others flooded. As a result, many miners never regained employment and by 1927 250,000 miners were out of work.

COAL INDUSTRY IN THE 1930s

Reduced Demand for Coal
By 1930 the coal industry faced many problems. The reduction in demand for coal was steady.

Lady Victoria Colliery, Newtongrange

Sorting the coal at the surface.

roof fall, cage and lift accidents and gas explosions were still present, though thankfully rarer. The age for going down the pit had been raised to 14 and no women worked underground. The length of the working day, although lengthened in 1926, was still a good deal shorter than the 12 hour shifts of the 1830s. The rates of pay varied from area to area but the minimum rate was retained. Generally, the level of pay had not improved even though the miners' standard of living had improved greatly. The isolation of the mine villages had been reduced thanks to transport improvements. The coming of council houses had begun to diminish the role of the owner as landlord as well and the hated truck system had disappeared.

There were too many small mines owned by different people, there being 1,000 different owners for the 2,000 mines in Britain. Neither the miners nor the owners could justify the investment necessary to introduce new technology. While the European countries vastly improved productivity in the post war years (by 40% or more) productivity in Britain rose by only 3%. The Samuel Commission, which was established to look into the industry, came to the conclusion that amalgamations of Coal Companies were necessary and the Mining Industry Act tried to persuade them to do this. In 1930 the Coal Mines Act established a Commission to encourage amalgamation. From 1927 onwards there were some successes. There were 38 amalgamations involving 369 mines and 240,000 miners. There was investment in new machinery, so that by 1938 more than half of the coal mined was cut and carried mechanically. This led to a

26% increase in productivity. On the other hand, it also led to a reduction in the number of miners employed from 1.2 million in 1923 to 0.75 million in 1938.

Work in the Mines in 1930

How had employment and working conditions changed in the coal industry over the century? With the coming of machinery the work was certainly easier for those who worked in the pits. Nevertheless, because of the lack of investment, more than half of the coal mined in Britain was still cut by hand. Overall, the miners were safer thanks to the technological advances which had been made. However, the new machinery, the deeper mines and the new techniques created new dangers and difficulties of their own.

There were, on average, more than 250,000 accidents in the coal mines each year in the 1920s. The dangers of flooding,

The Miners Union, despite being weakened by the General Strike, remained a powerful organisation, which was much respected by the miners. It continued to press for better pay and conditions. The standard of health of the miners remained a problem.

New machinery created more dust and more lung disease. Safety clothing was only being introduced in the 1930s—for example, the protective helmet. As a consequence of the falling demand for coal and the pit closures and amalgamations, there was quite a high level of unemployment. This was a new problem for the miners. At least in previous years there had been plenty of work—unpleasant as it may have been.

Despite all the changes over the 100 year period, coal mining remained an extremely difficult, dangerous and physically demanding job.

EVALUATION EXERCISE

coal mining

The following activities refer to the information given in Sources A—E.

Source A describes working conditions in a coal mine in Alloa. It was written by Robert Bald, a mining engineer, early in the 19th century.

IN those collieries where this mode is in practice, the collier leaves his house for the pits about eleven o'clock at night (attended by his sons, if he has any sufficiently old), when the rest of mankind are retiring to rest. Their first work is to prepare coals, by hewing them down from the wall. In about three hours after, his wife (attended by her daughters, if she has any sufficiently grown) sets out for the pit, having previously wrapped her infant child in a blanket, and left it to the care of an old woman who, for a small gratuity, keeps three or four children at a time, and who, in their mothers' absence, feeds them with ale or whisky mixed with water. The children who are a little more advanced are left to the care of a neighbour; and under such treatment, it is surprising that they ever grow up or thrive.

The mother, having thus disposed of her younger children, descends the pit with her older daughters when each, having a basket of a suitable form, lays it down, and into it the large coals are rolled; and such is the weight carried, that it frequently takes two men to lift the burden upon their backs: the girls are loaded according to their strength. The mother sets out first, carrying a lighted candle in her teeth; the girls follow, and in this manner they proceed to the pit bottom, and with weary steps and slow, ascend the stairs, halting occasionally to draw breath, till they arrive at the hill or pit-top, where the coals are laid down for sale; and in this manner they go for eight or ten hours almost without resting. It is no uncommon thing to see them, when ascending the pit, weeping most bitterly from the excessive severity of the labour; but the instant they have laid down their burden on the hill, they resume their cheerfulness, and return down the pit singing.

The execution of work performed by a stout woman in that way is beyond conception. For instance, we have seen a woman, during the space of time above mentioned, take on a load of at least 170 pounds avoirdupois, travel with this 150 yards up the slope of the coal below ground, ascend a pit by stairs 117 feet, and travel up on the hill 20 yards more to where the coals are laid down. All this she will perform no less than twenty four times as a day's work ... The weight of coals thus brought to the pit top by a woman in a day amount to 4,080 pounds or above 36 hundred-weight English, and there have been frequent instances of two tons being carried. The wages paid for this work are eightpence per day!—a circumstance as surprising almost as the work performed ...

From this view of the work performed by bearers in Scotland, some faint idea may be formed of the slavery and severity of the toil, particularly when it is considered that they are entered to this work when seven years of age, and frequently continue till they are upwards of fifty, or even sixty years old.

The collier, with his wife and children, having performed their daily task, return home, where no comfort awaits them; their clothes are frequently soaked with water and covered with mud; their shoes so very bad as scarcely to deserve the name. In this situation they are exposed to all the rigours of winter, the cold frequently freezing their clothes.

On getting home, all is cheerless and devoid of comfort; the fire is generally out, the culinary utensils dirty and unprepared, and the mother naturally seeks first after her infant child, which she nurses even before her pit clothes are thrown off.

"Light your lamp. This way—mind the hutches." He led and I stumbled after.

Even here, twelve hundred feet down, there was the same deafening, clattering roar as above. Races of six, eight, nine and ten hutches came rattling out of the black passages drawn by fast-going ponies, guided by a single rope which took the place of reins. Wee boy drivers, not so high as the undersized ponies some of them, grotesque in their patched, muddy clothes, cried in piercingly shrill voices at the animals, deep-chested men shouted back and forth as they rolled the coal-weighted hutches off the rails onto the smooth sheet plates and then onto the cages, or jerked the empty ones back to the rails.

"Follow this man, and without a word my new guide, a grizzled old miner, turned abruptly to the right down a dark passage—a 'level'— where the last echoes of the noisy pit bottom were quickly lost and only the weird babbling swish of an unseen stream and the sucking of the mucky ooze beneath our feet was audible."

Source B describes working conditions in a Fife coal mine. It was written by an American, Kellog Durland, in 1904.

NOTICE

IN CONSEQUENCE OF THE ACT OF THE 5TH AND 6TH QUEEN VICTORIA, CAP. 99, HIS GRACE THE DUKE OF HAMILTON HEREBY INTIMATES, THAT FROM AND AFTER THE 10TH CURRENT, NO *FEMALES*, UNDER 18 YEARS OF AGE, NOR AFTER THE 1ST OF MARCH NEXT, SHALL ANY *FEMALES*, OF WHATEVER AGE, BE EMPLOYED IN THE UNDERGROUND OPERATIONS AT REDDING COLLIERY. HE FARTHER INTIMATES, THAT FROM AND AFTER THE 1ST DAY OF MARCH NEXT, NO *MALE* PERSONS, UNDER THE AGE OF 10 YEARS, SHALL BE EMPLOYED UNDERGROUND AT SAID COLLIERY; AND HE STRICTLY PROHIBITS ALL HIS COLLIERS AND WORKMEN, AT SAID COLLIERY, FROM, IN ANY WAY, TAKING THE ASSISTANCE OF ANY SUCH IN THE UNDERGROUND OPERATIONS WHICH ARE BEING PERFORMED BY THEM.

(SIGNED) **JOHN JOHNSTON,** MANAGER

REDDING COLLIERY,
1st November, 1842.

Source C This notice was posted outside Redding Colliery, Falkirk in 1842.

Questions

1   Read Source A. How accurate is this description of working conditions in Scottish coal mines in the 1820s?

2   Read Source B. Compare this source with the previous one. What evidence is given of changes in working conditions?

3   How useful is Source C for learning about changes in employment in the Scottish coal industry in the mid-nineteenth century?

4   To what extent does Source E given an accurate picture of the truck system in Scotland?

5   How reliable is Source D for learning about living conditions in a miners row?

6   What problems do those who live in the rows have to face?

About this time (1868) we get some detailed revelations regarding the method of robbing the miner, known as the truck system. The miner was compelled to purchase his goods from the coal owner's shop or store; no other shop or store was allowed to open in the vicinity, and any thrifty housewife who sought to purchase her goods in some neighbouring town discovered that her husband or her son was promptly discharged from his employment. At Baillieston truck shop goods were 20% dearer than goods elsewhere; at Chapelhall a truck shop manager died worth £10,000, which indicates something of the profits made, inasmuch as most of that sum would be extra robbery on his own account after the coal owner had been satisfied.

Source D. This source was written by Tom Johnston, a Labour MP, in a book called *The History of the Working Classes in Scotland*. It was published in 1929.

In the Maryhill district of Glasgow there are often drains and two large ashpits in front of the colliers' houses: no chimney cans: roofs 6 or 7 feet from the floor. Of another row we are told there is no closet and the only way to improve it is to sweep it away. At the Red Toon owned by the Jordanhill Company, the gables incline outward and probably would tumble down altogether but for insecure buttresses. At Netherton there is a great stink...misery of disease...houses below level of ground. At Blairdardie whooping cough and eye disease is prevalent. At Carfin the cooking water comes from one of Dixon's pits and is imperfectly filtered. At Slamannan some floors were simply soft clay. At Garston the houses are so damp that passing a hand across the wall brings off water and paint and lime.

Source E is taken from *The History of the Working Classes in Scotland* by Tom Johnston MP. It was published in 1929. It describes living conditions in a miners row as quoted in a *Glasgow Herald* investigation in 1875.

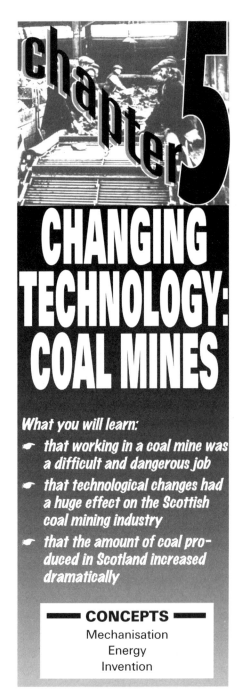

chapter 5

CHANGING TECHNOLOGY: COAL MINES

What you will learn:

☞ that working in a coal mine was a difficult and dangerous job

☞ that technological changes had a huge effect on the Scottish coal mining industry

☞ that the amount of coal produced in Scotland increased dramatically

CONCEPTS
Mechanisation
Energy
Invention

THE FIRST people to make regular use of coal and to work the deposits were the monks who settled in Scotland in the twelfth century. Monks from Newbattle Abbey near Dalkeith were among the earliest users. Quantities obtained in those early years were very small. One early use of coal was in saltpanning ie. boiling sea water to extract the salt. Famous centres for this were the towns of Prestonpans and Saltcoats. Coal was not initially used much for domestic fuel because people thought it was dangerous and smelly.

Early History

Early mining consisted of picking away at exposed coal deposits on the surface. The deposits would be removed until flooding or lack of decent ventilation stopped the work. Early shaft workings were called bell pits and they extracted coal as best they could without props until it became too dangerous. When that happened, the mine was abandoned and another shaft was opened nearby.

The first method of mining along a substantial level was the Pit and Adit method which improved ventilation and drainage. Coal was extracted by a miner using a pick and shovel. Shafts were also dug down to these levels and mining as we would recognise it today began. Coal was taken to the surface by women and children, who were known as bearers, and was carried up the shaft by a series of ladders, or sometimes by a simple windlass. In pits where gas was a problem and naked lights were too dangerous, a glow could be obtained by leaving rotting fish to give off a phosphorescent glow—and no little smell!

By 1500 coal production in Scotland was in the region of 40,000 tons. This came from all over Scotland and represented the produce of lots of small collieries. Pits were no more than 30 metres underground, though in Fife some coal mines were extended under the sea. Near Culross a shaft was opened below the high water mark allowing coal to be shipped away more easily.

By 1700, 500,000 tons were being produced annually. However, the early 1700s, after the Act of Union in 1707, was a fairly stagnant time in the history of Scottish coal mining. The coming of James Watt's steam engine in 1768 to the Burn Pit, Kinneil, was to prove to be the catalyst for more major change. This engine could power a variety of machines in the pit and the Industrial Revolution in coal mining was really underway. Flooded seams could be pumped out or kept dry. In addition, fresh air could be pumped down into deeper mines and mine shafts could be dug to a much greater depth.

At the same time the iron industry began to develop in Scotland, and with the discovery by

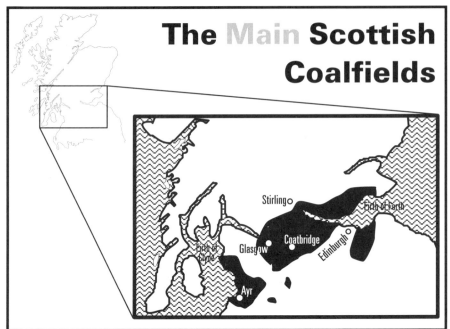

The Main Scottish Coalfields

Stirling
Firth of Forth
Coatbridge
Firth of Clyde
Glasgow
Edinburgh
Ayr

Abraham Derby that 'coked' coal could be used in the manufacture of iron, the demand for coal soared. In 1760 the Carron Iron works opened in Scotland. The Industrial Revolution depended on coal as its source of energy.

By 1830, the start of our period, the coal industry in Scotland was well established and coal was in ever increasing demand. The main sources of demand were

- domestic use — this was of growing importance in the industrial towns

- steam engine — as these were used to power factories as well as trains and other things, so the demand for coal grew

- industrial processes — eg. the iron industry, the glass industry, breweries etc

- limestone burning — for use in the growing agricultural industry

- exports — to Northern Europe from Lothian and Fife and to Ireland from the West of Scotland.

In 1830, using very primitive methods, about 3 million tons of coal were produced annually. In Scotland however, there was a great demand for more. The only way to achieve this was to go deeper, and to have mine seams at a greater distance from the shaft. To achieve this there had to be considerable technological developments and these occurred in all areas of the coal industry.

Locating the Coal Seams
Test drilling was necessary to locate good seams of coal. The Geological Survey was established in 1835. This surveyed the

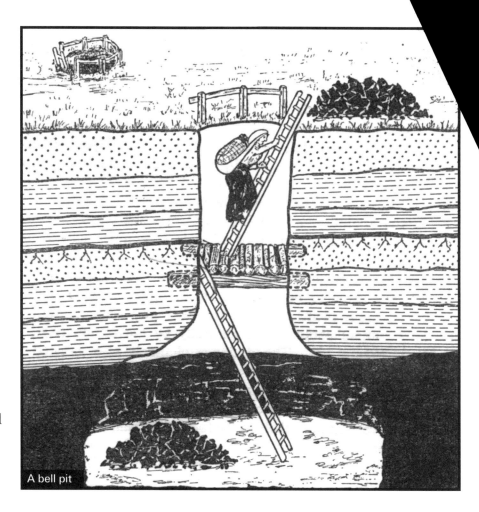

A bell pit

geology of Britain and, among other things, pinpointed likely sources of coal. Test drilling was made much easier in the 1830s with the development of the rotary drill, which cut out a solid column of rock as it drilled down. This could be extracted and examined scientifically. Previously, drills had crunched up the rock rather like a modern masonry drill and this had made accurate analysis more difficult. Core drilling became even faster in the 1870s with the introduction of diamond toothed rotary drills.

Opening a Mine
The first stage was to dig a shaft. Initially this was a square hole dug in the ground. As the depths became greater this was lined— at first with wood and later with brick or concrete. Once the shaft had been dug to the required depth and had exposed the seams, extraction could begin. In the early years of the twenti-

eth century wide circular shafts were dug providing extra space for ventilation.

Mining the Coal
Strangely enough this, the key process, showed the least technological development during the period. The miner, with pick and shovel and occasional blasting, was the main method used throughout the period. In 1913, 92% of all coal extracted in Britain was removed by pick and shovel, falling to 60% by 1936.

The first coal cutter—a sort of circular saw—was developed in 1843, but it was hand powered and so was of limited success. In 1864, Baird & Company of Coatbridge produced the 'Gartsherrie' machine. This was like a giant chainsaw with tough metal 'picks' for teeth. It could undercut about 200 metres of coal face to a depth of 1.5 metres in the space of six hours. However, even this machine had lim-

Advertising material for mechanised coal cutter.

ited use until tough enough metals could be developed to make the machine withstand the strain of the work.

Ventilation

The atmosphere in the coal mine was often stuffy and hot. There was also the ever present danger of poisoning or explosion from the gases trapped in the coal. The answer to these problems was found to be better ventilation. Early solutions involved digging two shafts and lighting a fire at the bottom of one to create a through draught. Huge fans were later installed—the first near Paisley in 1827. These could either extract stale air or else pump in fresh air. The use of fans, however, did not become widespread until the beginning of the 20th century.

Moving the Coal Underground

The use of children to drag coal from the face to the shaft ceased early in the period. Early improvements came with the wheeled 'hutches' which were much easier to move. In places where the shafts were high enough, horses were used. Shetland ponies were particularly popular because of their compact size. These remained in use until the mid-1960s. Where the

shaft was on a slope, gravity powered transport was developed using a pulley. The weight of the full hutches travelling downhill pulled the empty wagons back to the face. However, this could only be used in a limited number of areas. The next stage in development was the use of a steam engine to pull a continuous rope to which wagons could be attached. This system was introduced in 1844 and remained the commonest system of operation throughout the period. The hutches ran on rails.

At the turn of the century another development introduced at the coal face was the endless conveyor and conveyor belt. This took the coal from the cutting point to the loading area. The earliest of these was a chain fixed to a series of scrapers which dragged the coal along a trough. This was later modified to be a belt on which the coal was carried.

Lifting the Coal

The two great technological developments over the period were the introduction of wire rope about 1850 and steam winding engines which were first introduced into Lanarkshire. Using wire rope instead of hemp meant that greater loads could be lifted from greater depths. Steam winding engines replaced horse or water powered lifting mechanisms, or even human

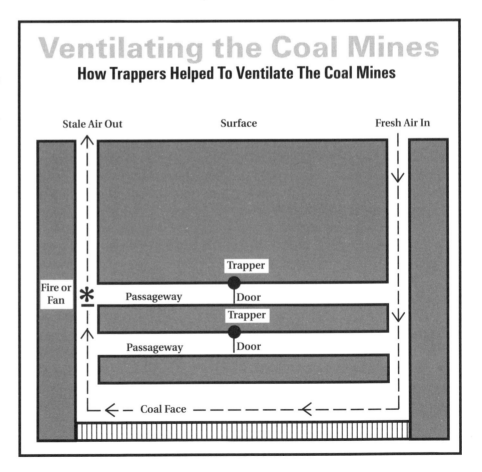

Ventilating the Coal Mines
How Trappers Helped To Ventilate The Coal Mines

58

Lifting

COAL FROM A MINE

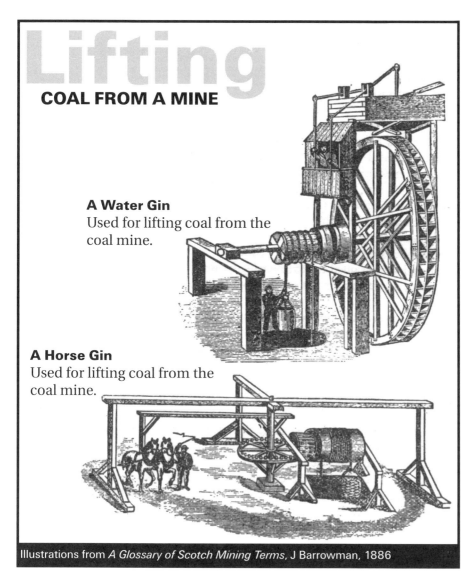

A Water Gin
Used for lifting coal from the coal mine.

A Horse Gin
Used for lifting coal from the coal mine.

Illustrations from *A Glossary of Scotch Mining Terms*, J Barrowman, 1886

muscle power. This increased the amount of coal which could be extracted from 250 tons to 600 tons per day. Operating the winding machine was a very responsible job and any accidents in the shaft were very serious. In 1842 an Act of Parliament set the minimum age for a winding engine operator at 15.

Pumping out the Mines

As mines grew deeper so the problems of water increased and keeping the mines clear of water was a constant task. Originally steam engines were used, often operating above ground, but they were not reliable and were very difficult to maintain. They did not cope well with pumping water from great depths. Only with the introduction of electricity did this particular task become easier.

Sources of Energy

Aside from the power of human muscle, the only source of energy in use at the beginning of the period was steam power. Much of the work done to develop steam engines was connected with mines. In some cases the steam boilers were located underground but this was very dangerous and, instead, the boiler was often placed at the top of the shaft and the steam was piped down to engines working below. This system remained in use until the turn of the century, although in some cases, ropes and belts from an engine at the top of the shaft worked the machinery at the bottom of the shaft. Nevertheless, steam power had many problems, not least heat loss and leakages through the pipes—especially where the engine was at the surface.

In 1849 an air compressor was installed in a coal mine at Govan Colliery near Glasgow. This could work machinery up to half a mile distant from the compressor and worked pumps and haulage machinery. The air travelled through cast iron pipes. The system worked well. However, it was at least 30 years later before the use of compressed air became widespread. Compressed air was an excellent source of energy for coal cutters. The famous 'Gartsherrie' cutter was powered by it. Yet, by 1900 only 30% of coal cut in Scotland was cut by machinery. By 1920, with technological developments widespread, this figure had risen to 34%. By 1930 most coal cutters were powered by compressed air, although electric power was being introduced.

The most significant change in sources of energy came with the developments in electricity. The first mains electrical lighting system was installed in Earnock Colliery, Hamilton, in 1881 and in 1891 an electrically driven coal cutter was supplied to Elphinstone Colliery, Tranent. There were dangers however, since sparks created by the electric power could set off an explosion of flammable gases. In 1912 it became compulsory for all electrical equipment used in mines to be designed and manufactured to certain safety standards. These were then awarded an official flame-proof stamp. From then on the use of electricity, for all tasks in the coal mines, spread rapidly.

SAFETY IN THE MINES

Coal mining was and is a very dangerous industry. As the demand for coal grew and mines became deeper, so the dangers increased. The technology acted here as a double-edged sword. On the one hand technological advances, for example new machinery, created their own new dangers. On the other hand there were significant developments which increased safety in the mines.

Roof Fall

It is essential to prop up the roof of the coal workings adequately. Initially this was done by leaving coal supports—the room and stoop method. During the 19th century this method was replaced by 'artificial' props. These might have to withstand pressures of 40 tons or more. Stronger props made either of wood or steel were used and latterly hydraulic props which could absorb movements in the roof were introduced.

Gas

There were three main types of gas, each of which presented unique problems. (See 'Dangerous Gases'.) Better ventilation dealt with many of these gases. However, there were other technological advances during the period which also contributed. Perhaps the most famous was the safety lamp invented by Sir Humphrey Davy in 1815. This worked by surrounding the flame with wire gauze, allowing air in to let the flame burn but not allowing it to ignite gases outside the gauze. The presence of inflammable gases was indicated by a change in the colour of the flame. However, this lamp did not give as much illumination as naked lights like candles and these were still being used in the 1850s and 1860s in mines where no risk of explosions was anticipated. In the years between 1835 and 1850 more than six hundred fires and explosions were reported in British coal mines. The Davy lamp was refined and improved, but the

Dangerous Gases

Black Damp

The commonest gas in the early mines was Block Damp. It was nonpoisonous and noninflammable. However, it reduced the amount of oxygen available in the mine and could result in asphyxiation of the miners. Good ventilation helped to clear this threat. Lighting a fire at the bottom of a shaft to create ventilation in the form of a draught was often used.

Fire Damp

This was highly flammable methane gas. This had always been around in mines, but as they grew deeper so it became more common and more dangerous. One early method of dealing with this hazard was to send down one very brave man in water soaked clothing. He entered the mine first each day with a naked light and burned off any quantities of the gas which had built up overnight. As the pits grew deeper and larger this became a less and less acceptable practice.

White Damp

The third gas, white damp or choke damp, is carbon monoxide. This is colourless and odourless and is therefore difficult to detect. However, the gas is very poisonous and it was necessary to ensure that it was not present. One early method of detecting the presence of this gas was to take a small creature like a mouse or a canary down the mine. They would show the effect of the gas quite quickly by collapsing, thus enabling the humans to evacuate the area before the gas built up to serious levels.

Beam engine, known to Ayrshire miners as 'Auld Ben'.

Roslin Colliery Rescue Brigade, circa 1910.

problem of lighting in the coal mines was not fully resolved until the development of the electric safety lamp.

Other Hazards

Other dangers in the mine were also addressed during the century. Transport of men and coal underground was steadily improved and dangerous practices were eliminated. Similarly in the shafts, the winding gear was refined and developed to ensure that there were few accidents. The presence of dense coal dust in the mines was recognised as a hazard early on. Any mining operation whether by explosive or pick, was bound to cause dust. As this was breathed in by the miners it caused severe irritation to the lungs and miner's lung and emphysema became a major health hazard. One method of dealing with this was to spray water over the affected area to damp down the dust. This was perhaps the most ironic development of all. At the start of the period great efforts were being made to pump mines dry, while by the end water was actually being pumped back down into them.

As the pace of mine development grew during the century, so another danger became apparent. The coal workings had many miles of old shafts honeycombing them. Nobody knew exactly where they all were. There was always a risk of breaking into old, flooded workings which would then flood the new mine, drowning or trapping any miners unfortunate enough to be there. An Act of Parliament in 1850 made it compulsory for each mine to prepare and register a Plan of the mine workings. Despite all the advances in safety, coal mining remained a very dangerous occupation and accidents caused by explosion, fire, roof fall, flooding, mechanical fault or human error were fairly common and usually quite serious.

MINES IN 1930

What was it like in a typical coal mine in 1930 and how had the impact of technology affected conditions? Firstly, mines were deeper underground. Many of the seams close to the surface had been worked out and a typical mine might be more than 1,000 feet deep. Movement up and down the shaft was by lifts and cages driven either by steam power or by electricity. Some coal was still mined using human muscle power, but machine cutting was becoming more common, although miners still had to be at the coalface to guide and operate the machines. The height of the coal seams might still have been uncomfortably low, but the roof would be supported by carefully placed pit props of which the most modern were hydraulic. The coal would be moved from the face to the bottom of the shaft either by conveyor belt or by wagons running on tracks. Often these would be pulled by horses, but in other mines they would be worked by systems of ropes and pulleys, powered by steam, compressed air or maybe electricity. Mines were largely lit by electric power or by the use of safety lamps. They were ventilated by large fans which drew in fresh air and pumped out stale air and gases.

Women and children no longer worked in the mines. The earliest age a boy could begin work down a mine was now 14. The length of a shift down a mine had been reduced to 8–10 hours on average. Wages, in relative terms, were not as high as they once had been since the demand for coal was not as high as it had been twenty years before. There had been unpleasant strikes in the mines in 1923 and 1926, resulting in the wages being cut and the working day being lengthened.

After the First World War the export market was all but eliminated, while the development of new sources of energy meant that the demand for coal was beginning to fall. Nevertheless, comparisons with 1830 would show a huge increase in produc-

Winding tower at Lady Victoria Colliery.

tion and in the number of men employed. The work in the mines was not as physical as it had been in 1830 as machines did much of the heavy work. On the face of it, technological developments had been good to the coal industry, enabling it to produce more, from greater depths, in greater safety and at a reduced cost. Technological developments in other industries like iron and steel and the railways had increased the demand for coal. On the other hand, further developments in technology were identifying other sources of energy, for example oil, which were, eventually, to damage the coal industry.

EVALUATION EXERCISE

changing technology: coal mines

The following activities refer to the information given in Sources A—H.

Sources A and B are taken from the *Report of the Royal Commission on Coal Mines* in 1842.

Source A is from evidence given by a Wolverhampton doctor.
Source B was written by a visitor to a coal mine in the West Riding of Yorkshire.

Source A

"The colliers are so healthy that wounds and large gashes are cured with a rapidity quite surprising; compound fractures are cured with scarcely a troublesome symptom. As to formation, the collier, as he walks, rolls along, swinging at the hips as if he were double jointed; the manufacturer creeps along as if his bones were all huddled together." (*Parliamentary Papers, 1842,* Vol. XV, p. 14.)

Source B

"I have often been shocked in contemplating the hideous and anything but human appearance of these men, who are generally found in a state of bestial nakedness, lying their whole length on the uneven floor, and supporting their heads upon a board or short crutch; or sitting upon one heel balancing their persons by extending the other. Black and filthy as they are in their low, dark, heated and dismal chambers, they look like a race fallen from the common stock. It did not much surprise me to be told that old age came prematurely upon them; indeed the careworn countenances, the grey hair and furrowed brows I met with at that age were sufficient indications of that fact." (*Parliamentary Papers, 1842.* Vol. XII, App.: Pt. II, pp. 63–4.)

Source C
Girls carrying coal in an East of Scotland coal mine. Circa 1840.

Average Weekly Wages in Coal Mines, Bradford and Leeds 1842

Age of Child	Wage
5	2s/6d (12.5p)
6	2s/6d (12.5p)
7	2s/8d (13p)
8	3s/0d (15p)
9	3s/5d (17.5p)
10	4s/0d (20p)
11	4s/7d (23p)
12	5s/4d (27p)
13	6s/4d (33p)
14	7s/2d (36p)
15	7s/10d (39p)
16	8s/7d (43p)
17	10s/3d (53p)

Source D

Sources D—F are taken from the *Report of the Royal Commission on Coal Mines* in 1842. They are related to the work done by children.

Source E

There is evidence that some children begin work in the pits of the Coalbrook Dale district as early as six years of age. One instance indeed came under the observation of the sub-Commissioner, in which a child two years younger, that is four years of age, was regularly taken into the pit by his father. "This remarkable instance became known to me," says Dr Mitchell. "When exploring the Hills Lane pit, the ground-bailiff and a labouring collier accompanied me." "I say, Jones," said the ground-bailiff to one of the charter-masters, "there are very few children working in this mine: I think we have none under ten or eleven." The collier immediately said, "Sir, my little boy is only a little more than four." This was a very unseasonable interruption and all the ground-bailiff said was, "Well, I suppose you take good care of him: you take him down and up when you go yourself." (*Parliamentary Papers, 1842.* Vol. XV, p 9.)

Source F

The children that excite the greatest pity are those who stand behind the doors to open and shut them: they are called trappers, who in the darkness, solitude and stillness as of night, eke out a miserable existence for the smallest of wages. I can never forget the first unfortunate creature that I met with: it was a boy of about eight years old, who looked at me as I passed with an expression the most abject and idiotic—like a thing, a creeping thing, peculiar to the place. On approaching and speaking to him he shrank trembling and frightened into a corner.
(*Parliamentary Papers, 1842,* Vol. XV, p 72.)

Coal Production in the UK
Before and after the First World War

Source G Figures for British coal production before and after the First World War.

Questions

1 What evidence is there of disagreement between sources A and B? Can you account for it?

2 Use Sources C–F. What were working conditions like for children in coal mines in the years before 1842?

3 Study Source G. What changes in coal production can be seen from the graph? Account for the changes.

4 Study Source H. What evidence is there that coal mining became safer between 1830 and 1939?

The Principal Scottish Mining Disasters

Year	Pit Area	Area	Accident	Number killed/injured
1846	Bogle Hole	Lanarkshire	Not detailed	6 killed
1847	Drumpellier	Lanarkshire	Not detailed	3 killed
1851	Nitshill	Renfrewshire	Explosion	61 killed
1876	Cadzow	Lanarkshire	Explosion	Not known
1877	Home Farm	Lanarkshire	Flooding from old workings	4 killed
1877	Blantyre	Lanarkshire	Explosion	207 killed
1878	Barwood	Stirlingshire	Explosion	17 killed
1879	Blantyre	Lanarkshire	Explosion	25 killed
1887	Udston	Lanarkshire	Explosion	73 killed
1888	Morningside	Lanarkshire	Drowning	1 killed
1889	Mauricewood	Lothian	Fire	63 killed
1893	Herbertshire	Lanarkshire	Explosion	2 killed
1895	Auchenharvie	Ayrshire	Flooding	9 killed
1895	Quarter	Stirlingshire	Explosion	13 killed
1895	Kinneddar	Fife	Fire	9 killed
1897	Devon	Clackmannan	Flooding from old workings	6 killed
1898	Drumpellier	Lanarkshire	Explosion	4 killed
1901	Donibristle	Fife	Flooding from old workings	8 killed
1907	Dalbeath	Fife	Roof collapse	1 killed
1909	Arniston	Lothian	Powder magazine explosion	Not known
1913	Cadder	Lanarkshire	Fire	22 killed
1917	Springhill	Ayrshire	Explosion	4 killed
1918	Stanrigg	Lanarkshire	Inrush of moss	19 killed
1922	East Plean	Stirlingshire	Explosion	12 killed
1923	Redding	Stirlingshire	Flooding from old workings	23 killed
1923	Gartshore	Dumbartonshire	Explosion	8 killed
1925	Shawfield	Lanarkshire	Winding accident	4 killed
1930	Auchinraith	Lanarkshire	Explosion	6 killed
1934	Polmaise	Stirlingshire	Explosion	3 killed
1938	Dumbreck	Stirlingshire	Fire	9 killed
1939	Valleyfield	Fife	Explosion	33 killed

Source H Compiled by the Scottish Mining Museum.

chapter 6

THE RAILWAYS

What you will learn:

- that railways played an important part in the industrial revolution
- that railways expanded rapidly from the 1840s onwards
- that people could move around more easily which affected where they lived and worked
- that railways made many new leisure activities possible

CONCEPTS

Industry
Technology
Railway Mania
Standard of living
Social change

WHEN, IN 1748, the Provost of Glasgow and two colleagues went to London to see members of the government, they had to buy their own horse-drawn coach because there was no coach service from Glasgow to London. The journey took them twelve days and cost over £25, a huge sum in those days. It is hard for us to realise just how difficult it was for people to travel around in the 18th century. We can travel the length of

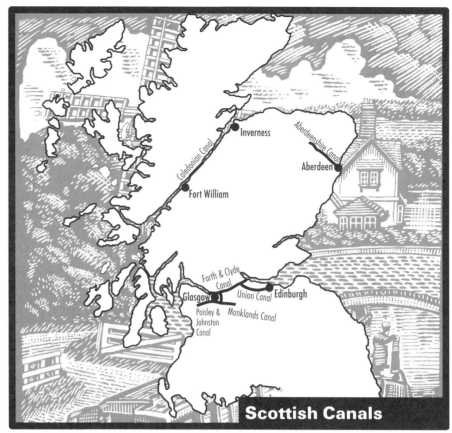

Scottish Canals

Britain in a day by car or bus and reach anywhere in Europe by plane in a few hours. In 1750 the coach service from Edinburgh to London ran once a fortnight and took 12 to 16 days. Even Glasgow, just 46 miles away, took 12 hours to reach from Edinburgh by coach.

During the industrial revolution good transport became of vital importance for the new industries which were growing up. By the 1820s improvements in road building had made road travel much easier. The journey from Edinburgh or Glasgow to London now took a mere 3 to 4 days and coach services were running between most large towns.

However, coach travel was still expensive, and ordinary people would not use it unless they had to. Many people never travelled more than walking distance from their own town or village. For country people a visit to the nearest town was a special treat. In the growing industrial towns the lack of cheap transport

meant that people had to live within walking distance of their work. They had little choice but to make their homes in crowded slum tenements overshadowed by smoky factory chimneys.

Transporting goods by road was still a slow and costly process and this caused problems for industry. The owners of iron works and textile mills had to be able to get bulky raw materials to their factories and finished goods to the seaports. Loads like the coal which powered the new steam driven machinery were very awkward to deal with. The horse-drawn wagons which carried goods were slow and expensive so wherever possible heavy goods were sent by sea or river.

The demands of industry led to the building of a system of canals to extend the navigable waterways. In Scotland the canals linked Glasgow and Edinburgh with the main industrial areas in central Scotland. Journeys for coastal shipping were made shorter by the construction of the Crinan and Caledonian canals. A canal barge pulled by one horse could pull much more than a wagon pulled by four horses, so the cost of freight transport was more than halved.

However, canals were expensive to build, and travel on them was still quite slow. Obviously something better was needed if industry was to continue to expand. The answer to the problem was to build railways and by 1830 the first steps towards their development had already been taken in.

The First Railways

The idea of railway tracks was not new. Long before the 19th century, wagonways with wooden rails had been used to make it easier to move horse-drawn trucks, especially in mining areas. The wagonway which linked the coal mines of Tranent with the harbour at Port Seton was already 23 years old when some Jacobite troops used the track to attack the government army at the battle of Prestonpans in 1745—probably the first use of a railway in warfare. As industry grew so did the use of wagonways.

By the early 19th century new technological advances had made a major breakthrough possible. Improvements in iron making techniques meant that wooden rails were replaced with much stronger ones made of iron. Then came the steam engine—the work-horse of the industrial revolution. First developed by Thomas Newcomen in 1709, the steam engine was greatly improved by the Scottish engineer James Watt. Watt's steam engine could be adapted to turn all sorts of machinery, and soon attempts were being made to use it for a moving engine.

Several people, such as the

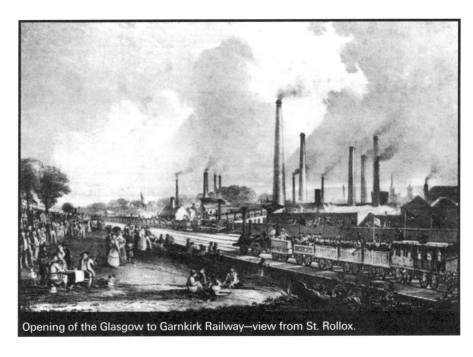
Opening of the Glasgow to Garnkirk Railway—view from St. Rollox.

Scotsman William Murdoch, experimented with steam driven road carriages, but they were heavy and clumsy and not a great success. It was an Englishman called Richard Trevithick who had the idea of putting the steam engine onto a railway track. In 1808 he publicised his invention with a steam locomotive which pulled trucks on a model railway in London. The idea was taken up by other engineers, notably George Stephenson from Northern England and his son Robert.

In 1825 the first ever public railway service was opened between Stockton and Darlington. The engineer who designed the line was Stephenson and the engine which pulled the trucks was his 'Locomotion'. It was such a success that soon plans were under way for a passenger line between Liverpool and Manchester. Stephenson was chief engineer for the line which was to run for 30 miles across some difficult country. The businessmen backing the new line wanted the best possible engine for it so they held a competition at Rainhill in 1829. Three engines competed for the prize.

Stephenson's 'Rocket' was the winner, reaching the speed of 29 miles per hour while pulling a loaded train. When the Liverpool to Manchester line was officially opened in 1830, it was Stephenson's engines which pulled the trains.

The new line was a great success. By 1831 it was carrying an average 1,250 passengers a day as well as hauling goods. Trains could travel at over 30 miles per hour, an amazing speed for the time! People discussed anxiously whether humans could survive even higher speeds without risk to life. For the first time there was a form of public transport which was not only much quicker than anything that had gone before, but was also cheap enough to be afforded by ordinary people. A new age of travel had begun. There were some opponents of the new railways. Obviously the stage-coach and canal operators were not happy. Landowners and farmers worried over the damage that might be done. Railways were dirty and noisy and cows, terrified by the new engines, might stop giving milk. Also, sparks from the smoke stacks might set houses on fire. Others were quick to see the advantages. Landowners whose land lay in the path of a new railway stood to make big profits and middle-class people saw the chance to get rich by investing their money in railways.

To build a new railway required an Act of Parliament. At first the government's policy was one of *laissez faire*—not interfering in what they saw as a matter for businessmen, not politicians. Dozens of schemes were put forward for Parliament's approval.

THE EXPANSION OF THE RAILWAYS

Scotland

Soon new lines were being opened or planned all over Britain. Scotland was well to the fore

in this. By 1817, one of Stephenson's engines had been tried out on the private Kilmarnock to Troon railway, built to link coal mines to the seaport. However, the engine was too heavy for the track which had been designed only for horse-drawn trucks. The first line designed to use locomotives was the Kirkintilloch to Monklands line which opened in 1826 to carry coal. Although it used horse-drawn trucks at first, by 1832 steam engines were in regular use on the line.

The first Scottish passenger service was the Garnkirk to Glasgow line which opened in 1831. The first train, driven by Stephenson himself, consisted of covered coaches for the richer passengers plus open trucks for other passengers. Railway travel was not at all comfortable for poorer passengers in the early days. Standing in the open trucks (seats were a luxury denied them), third class passengers were exposed both to the weather and to the smoke and cinders from the engine. Nevertheless, hundreds of people were willing to endure these hardships for the thrill of a ride on the railway. The lot of third class passengers was slightly improved by the 1844 Railway Act.

By the 1840s central Scotland had a network of railways. Many lines were built to serve the mines and iron works, but passenger lines were also very important. In 1842 the Edinburgh to Glasgow line was opened and immediately proved to be very popular. By 1846 it was carrying over a million people a year, the majority of whom were third class passengers. Other lines were built linking Glasgow with Paisley, Greenock, Kilmarnock and Ayr. In the east the North British company opened the Edinburgh to Berwick line in 1846, with a ferry link to the line

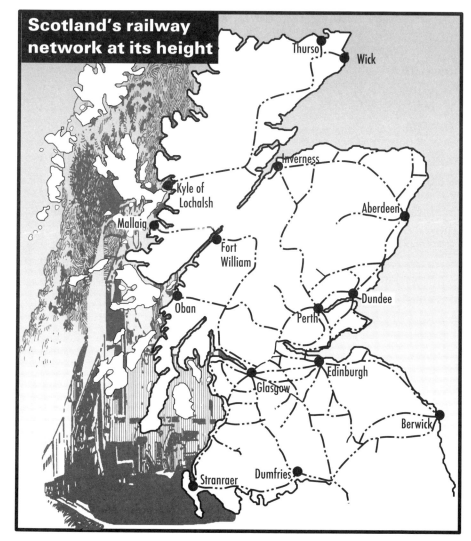

Scotland's railway network at its height

coming up from Newcastle. In 1848 the Caledonian line was opened from Carlisle to Carstairs with branches to both Edinburgh and Glasgow. Thus both cities were linked to London by rail.

By the 1850s southern Scotland was being opened up by a network of railways. The Waverley line, named after the novels of the great Borders writer Sir Walter Scott, reached Hawick in 1849 and in the next few years most of the Border towns were linked to the railway system. The Waverley line was extended to Carlisle in 1862. To the north, lines had been built to Stirling, Perth, Dundee, Montrose and Aberdeen, and in 1858 a line from Aberdeen linked up with the Inverness railway.

It took much longer to open up the Highlands. The difficult terrain and the lack of large population centres meant that it was very expensive to build and run railways. However, by 1874 a line had been completed from Inverness to Wick and Thurso in the far north. By 1880 there was a line from Glasgow to Oban on the west coast. The West Highland line to Fort William was completed by 1894, and when it was extended to Mallaig in 1901, this opened up ferry travel to the Western Isles.

By the early 1900s practically every Scottish town had its railway station. Sometimes railway companies developed lines which were never likely to be successful in economic terms in order to compete with a rival company or to satisfy the local desire for a rail link. A fine example of this was the Berwickshire line which opened in 1865 linking the east coast line with Duns and St Boswells. The North British Company's line from St Boswells to Tweedmouth, which

opened in 1851, already provided a service for the eastern Borders. Although branch lines like these might have run at a loss, they did feed customers into the profitable main-line railway systems.

England
In England, too, expansion was very rapid. Soon all the major towns and cities were linked up by a network of lines built by many different companies. By 1840 London was linked to Liverpool and Manchester and by 1844 another line was open from London to Newcastle. The Great Western Railway had linked London to Bristol by 1841. By 1845 over 2,000 miles of line were open with another 4,000 miles following in the next three years. In 1848 the North Western line linked with the Caledonian line to make it possible to travel from London to Glasgow by railway. The east coast route from Edinburgh to London was completed in 1850 when the Union Bridge, the work of Robert Stephenson, was opened at Berwick.

Gauges
One problem which had to be overcome was the question of gauge—the width of the track. For hundreds of years carts had been built with the wheels roughly 4.5 feet apart, so that they could follow the ruts made by other carts. Early railways tended to use a similar gauge, but there were wide variations. George Stephenson's tracks had a gauge of 4 feet 8.5 inches, but another of the railway builders of the time, Isembard Kingdom Brunel, used a gauge of 7 feet on his famous Great Western Railway. He claimed that it was smoother and safer. However, as the railway network grew it was clear that one gauge would have to be agreed on to save the passengers having to change trains every time they went onto an-

other company's line.

In 1846 the government intervened with the Railways Act saying that all railway companies must use the 4 feet 8.5 inches gauge on their new lines.

Railway Mania
During the 1840s many people became convinced that they could make their fortunes by investing in railway companies. By 1845 all sorts of schemes were being set up and the situation rapidly got out of hand. All over the country surveyors were busy marking out proposed new lines, often in the most unlikely places. Landowners made quick profits selling land to railway companies and thousands of people put their life savings into railway building.

Unfortunately many of the schemes were unsound and some were downright fraudulent with directors who fiddled the shareholders' money for their own private profit. By the end of 1845 the boom was collapsing. Many companies went bust and some people were driven to suicide by the disaster. The most dramatic collapse came in 1849 when the railway empire of George Hudson fell apart. He controlled many lines in the Midlands and north-west England, but went bust when it was discovered that he had misused company money.

After this, railway building continued at a more moderate rate, but the expansion continued steadily throughout our period of study. By 1910 Britain had 19,979 miles of railways and in 1930 they reached their maximum of 20,464 miles. Virtually every town in Britain had its railway station.

City Transport
In large cities suburban lines

were developed to provide transport for commuters from the outlying areas to the town centres. In London and Glasgow underground railways were run beneath the built-up city centre areas. There were obvious problems of ventilation when using steam engines underground. This was solved by using stationary engines to pull trains attached to a steel cable. By the 1930s electric trains were coming into use and proved to be very successful.

Another development was the use of trams—passenger transport run on tramways or rails along city streets. At first trams were horse-drawn, but by the 1900s electric power was being installed. Most large British cities had electric trams operating until the 1960s.

THE SOCIAL IMPACT OF THE RAILWAYS

From the very start railway travel was popular with the general public. This worried some of the upper classes who feared that it was dangerous to allow the common people to travel around. They might learn too much and get ideas above their station! There is no doubt that railways transformed the lives of the people. The coming of the railways ended the isolation of rural communities and made it possible, for the first time, for ordinary people to move around easily, for both work and pleasure.

Commuting
It was no longer essential for people to live cheek by jowl with the places where they worked. As public transport improved, commuting to work became the norm for thousands of workers. For example, the Singer factory at Clydebank had a large work force, who came to work each

day on specially timetabled trains. By the 1890s, as well as the main railway lines, Glasgow commuters could use the underground suburban railway. Cities spread rapidly as better-off white collar workers moved away from the crowded tenements of the city centres to the suburbs where they could have larger houses and gardens. The really rich—factory owners for instance—could live even further away in pleasant commuter towns like Helensburgh and Largs on the Clyde or North Berwick on the East Lothian coast.

Better Shopping
It became much easier to move fresh farm produce into the towns. With daily supplies of fresh milk, meat, fruit and vegetables the diet of town dwellers was greatly improved. Manufactured goods such as tinned foods, clothes and shoes, household furnishings and kitchenware could be brought from all over the country to be sold in the local shops—at prices most people could afford too. All

this helped to raise the standard of living.

In rural areas people no longer had to depend solely on locally produced goods. Better transport meant that the village shop would stock a much wider range of products. It was now possible to take the train to the nearest town or city for a day's shopping. The down side of this was that small craft-based businesses in the country disappeared as they could no longer compete with the factory produced goods which were now so readily available. The growth of the railways accelerated movement of the population from the country to the towns as country people became more aware of the attractions of town life.

Leisure
The way people spent their free time was also dramatically changed by the railways. Going away on holiday was no longer a pleasure reserved for the very few. Seaside resorts grew up where middle-class families

London North Eastern Railway Poster. The social impact of the railways.

could go for their summer holidays—places like North Berwick, St Andrews, Carnoustie, Largs and Ayr. Lodgings would be rented for the month, and the children could spend their time playing on the beach while Dad had his daily round on the local golf course. Small fishing communities were transformed as shops, hotels, cafes and entertainments were developed to cater for the thousands of summer holiday visitors.

The opening up of the Highland railways helped to make this area the playground of the rich. Queen Victoria set the fashion with her regular visits to Balmoral. Soon everybody who was anybody bought or rented their Highland estate where they would entertain large parties each summer at the grouse shooting or deer stalking. Great landowners might even have their own private station. The Duke of Sutherland, for example, had his own station at Dunrobin.

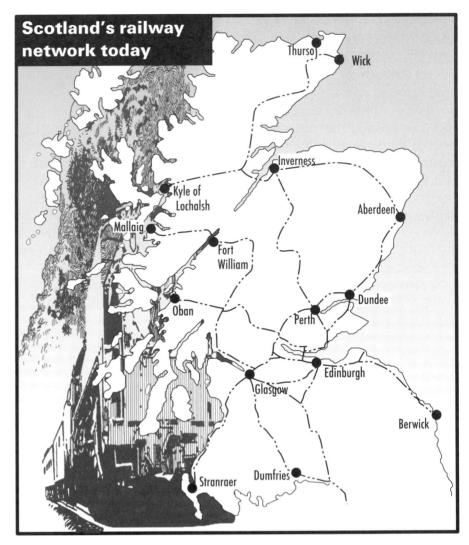

Scotland's railway network today

Sport was greatly influenced by the railways. We have already mentioned golf and hunting, but did you realise that the railways made football the game it is today? Of course football had been played by ordinary people for hundreds of years, but it was cheap railway transport which helped it to grow into a national sport. Railways made it possible for players and their supporters to travel to matches against other teams on Saturday afternoons. This meant that the sport had to be organised and so the football league developed to lay down national sets of rules and to draw up fixture lists. The first organised football club in Scotland was Queens Park, set up in 1867, and in 1873 the Scottish Football Association was formed. By 1900 there were over 100 clubs in the SFA including Hearts, Hibs, Celtic and Rangers.

The railway companies were well aware of the money to be made from tourism and ran excursions of all kinds. There were tours to the Burns country and the Scott country. The opening of the Union Bridge in 1850 came just in time to allow trains to be run from Scotland to London for the Great Exhibition of 1851. On Saturdays special trains were run to sporting events. During the Glasgow Fair each summer, thousands of people would be carried by train to Clyde resorts like Gourock and Ardrossan where they could catch ferries for a ride 'doon the watter'. The railway companies also got involved in running the ferries. The Caledonian Steam Packet Company, for instance, was an off-shoot of the Caledonian Railway Company.

Thus the leisure time of the na-

tion was transformed. Holidays became a normal feature of most peoples' lives. Even the poorest people might be able to enjoy a day trip to the seaside at least once a year. Many towns had an annual holiday to make this possible. Kelso in the Borders still has its Spittal Trip Day which started when the local churches decided to take advantage of the new railway opened in 1851 to take the children of the poor to the seaside. It was a far cry from the days when many people never went further than walking distance from their homes.

Time
One other small but important result of railways was the standardisation of time. Before this, clocks were usually checked by the sun at noon so there could be a big difference beween the

east and west of the country. In the days of coaches, journeys were so slow that it didn't really matter that the clocks in Bath were half an hour behind those in London. However, once you had trains running to a strict timetable it was essential for clocks to be the same all over the country. From December 1846 all station clocks were set at Greenwich mean time.

THE RAILWAYS IN THE 20TH CENTURY

The Effects of War
Before the First World War there were over 100 different railway companies in Britain. During the First World War the railways were so important for the war effort that they were taken under government control. Many lines suffered damage with no proper repairs except where the war effort made it necessary. When they were returned to private ownership, it was clear that the smaller pre-war companies could not finance the up-dating of the railway system which was needed. By the 1921 Railways Act the number of companies was reduced to four: the South-ern, the Great Western, the London Midland and Scottish, and the London and North-Eastern.

Between the Wars
In the 1920s and '30s the rail-ways' dominance of public transport still seemed to be beyond doubt. Improvements in engines continued and trains became faster and more comfortable. Average speeds of 90 mph became normal on express runs. The first experiments were being carried out with diesel and electric trains. Fares were kept low and freight transport was improved by the use of containers which reduced the amount of loading and unloading.

However, for the first time in a hundred years the railways had serious competition. Before World War I motor cars were luxury items, playthings of the rich, but the war gave a great boost to motor transport. When peace returned, hundreds of army lorries were sold off and were converted to peacetime use. Some were turned into buses which could provide a cheaper and more convenient form of transport than the railways. Mass production of motor cars, first pioneered by the American Henry Ford, was soon copied in Britain by firms like Morris and Austin. Cars were now cheap enough to be purchased by many middle-class families and motoring became a great new pastime.

Decline of the Railways
In 1930 the British railway system was at its maximum size. Since then it has been reduced to a shadow of its former glory. The damage and disruption caused by another war led to the nationalisation of the railways in 1948. British Railways, in the 1950s, tried to modernise with diesel and electric trains but, unable to compete with the booming motor transport industry, they had to close many lines. The biggest cuts came in the 1960s when, following a study by Dr Beeching, many branch lines disappeared and over 2,000 stations were closed. Today few towns have a railway station and only the main inter-city lines and some of the busier suburban lines have a secure future. Even now, there is a question mark over the future of the West Highland line and the route from Inverness to Thurso.

EVALUATION EXERCISE

the railways

Source A: LNER Poster

NORTH BERWICK — IT'S QUICKER BY RAIL

Illustrated Booklet free from Town Clerk or any L·N·E·R Agency

During the course of last week there has been a large amount of business transacted in our Exchange. Nearly all descriptions of Railway Shares were eagerly sought after and sales were made at much higher prices than last week. Speculators are eagerly enquiring after Shares in the Perth and InvernessRailway.

Source B is taken from the *Scottish Railway Gazette*, 12 April 1845.

Britain is at present an island of lunatics, all railway mad. The ultimate miracles of railways are obvious. The world is not half the size it was a few years ago. On the whole the results must be good. But the outrages of these (railway) speculators is frightful. Their principle is that nothing must obstruct their dividends. The margin of a loch, the course of a stream, a gentle valley the most brutal inroads are made on the most sacred of haunts.

Source C is taken from *The Journal Of Henry Cockburn*, A leading Scottish lawyer, 28 November 1845.

From the progress of the Railroads, all parts of the country will become more opened up. The artisan can, at little expense of time and money, bring out his materials and take home his work; and the man of business can as easily join his family at a distance of ten or twelve miles as at a distance of two. Wherever the railway goes fish will now be carried. The produce of the land, whether animal, vegetable or mineral, will with equal ease be brought to the coast.

Source D is from the *Scottish Railway Gazette*, 5 April 1845.

Questions

1 How useful is source B as evidence about 'Railway Mania'?

2 How far do the authors of Sources C and D agree about the consequences of the expansion of the railways?

3 How accurately do these three sources describe the effects of the expansion of the railways at this time?

4 How reliable is Source A as evidence that the railways had an effect on people's leisure activities?

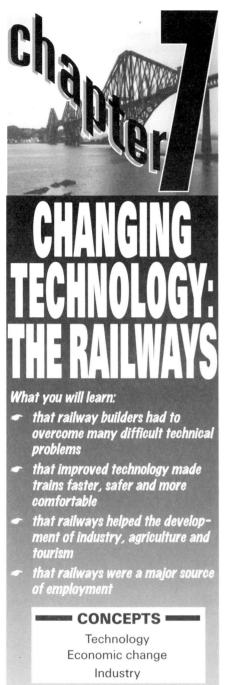

chapter 7

CHANGING TECHNOLOGY: THE RAILWAYS

What you will learn:

- ☞ *that railway builders had to overcome many difficult technical problems*
- ☞ *that improved technology made trains faster, safer and more comfortable*
- ☞ *that railways helped the development of industry, agriculture and tourism*
- ☞ *that railways were a major source of employment*

━━━ CONCEPTS ━━━
Technology
Economic change
Industry

LOOKING AT the work of the railway builders you cannot help being impressed. Railway engines cannot cope with steep hills, and so the lines had to be made as level as possible.

Building the Lines

When railway building started there was no machinery such as tractors or bulldozers to do the heavy work. It was not until the 1880s that steam cranes and diggers came into use. Most of our railways were built by men using picks, shovels, spades and barrows to shift the earth. With these basic tools and some gunpowder they managed some amazing engineering feats. The problems faced by Stephenson on the Manchester to Liverpool line were typical. The most difficult problem was Chat Moss, a peat bog too soft to bear the weight of man or horse. Stephenson's solution was to float the railway line across the Moss on wooden hurdles. To cross the gorge of the river Sankey he designed a viaduct of nine arches 70 feet high. At Edge Hill the line was carried through the Olive Mount Cutting, over two miles long and up to 100 feet deep. The Edinburgh to Glasgow line was another early engineering triumph. It included a thirty-six arch viaduct, designed by the famous Scottish engineer Telford, over the river Almond; several miles of cuttings through solid rock at Croy, Philpstoun and Bishopbriggs; and two tunnels at Falkirk and Winchburgh. All this produced 45 miles of almost perfectly level line. Unfortunately for the engineers of the E & G, the last mile and a half into Glasgow had to go down a steep gradient in a tunnel because the owners of the Forth and Clyde Canal would not allow the line to be carried over their canal on a bridge. This meant that trains had to be pulled up and down by stationary engines.

Another spectacular example of the work of the railway builders was the West Highland line which opened in 1894. Carved through some of the wildest land in Britain, it needed nineteen stone-built viaducts and one hundred and two bridges to carry the track across rivers and gorges and along the sides of mountains. The line had to cross Rannoch Moor, a desolate plateau rising up to 1,350 feet above sea level. The builders used Stephenson's technique of floating it on layers of brushwood to carry the line across the treacherous peat bogs of the moor. Five thousand men were employed on building the line. They created one of the world's most scenic railways.

Navvies

Wherever lines were laid, railway engineers faced similar problems. Fortunately, there was already a suitable work force available. The 'navigators' or 'navvies' who had dug the canals easily adapted to working on railways. Thousands of men were needed for the work and it was always an alarming experience for the local population when the navvies arrived. They were a tough

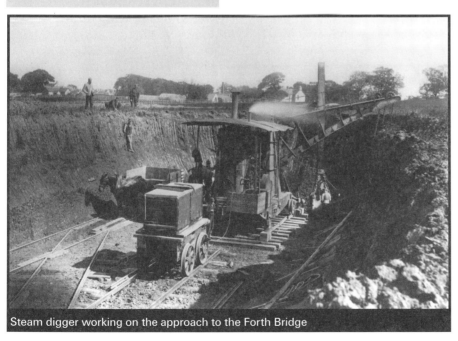

Steam digger working on the approach to the Forth Bridge

bunch of men, many of whom were Irishmen who had come to Britain to escape from the poverty of their own land. They lived in encampments of rough huts next to the line. The wages were usually high, but all too often they were spent on drinking sprees. Fights between rival bands of navvies were not uncommon.

Cuttings, Tunnels and Embankments

The work was extremely hard. Where cuttings could not be dug out with pick and shovel, gunpowder was used and the resulting rubble had to be shifted by men with barrows. Plank paths were laid up the sides of the cutting. The barrows were attached to ropes pulled by horses, but it was the navvies who had to guide the barrows up the slippery muddy planks. Tunnels were even more difficult and were usually dug in sections from vertical shafts dug down to the line of the tunnel. Embankments also required an enormous amount of labour to pile up the earth and rock to the required level. It was reckoned that a top navvy could fill and shift eight wagon-loads or about twenty tons of earth in a day. Navvying was hard and dangerous work and there were many accidents, some of which were fatal.

Railway cutting being dug

Bridges

Among the most striking achievements of the railway engineers were the viaducts and bridges which were built all over Britain to carry railways across rivers, gorges and estuaries. Many fine bridges were built in stone, like the Union Bridge at Berwick, opened in 1850, the elegant 19 arch bridge over the Tweed at Leaderfoot, or the 51.5 metre high viaduct over the river Ayr at Ballochmyle, reckoned to be the highest in Britain.

The advances in the iron and steel industry during the 19th century led to many bridges being constructed of metal. The most outstanding example of this has to be the world-famous Forth Bridge with its cantilever design (1890). Its massive structure, the largest of its type in Britain, was built to the highest safety standards. The designers, J Fowler and B Baker, did not want a repeat of the Tay Bridge disaster of 1879 which claimed 79 lives. The central span of the iron girder bridge collapsed in a storm, taking the Dundee express with it. The contractor for the West Highland line to Mallaig in 1901 was Robert McAlpine, an early pioneer of concrete construction, which was cheaper than stone and easier to maintain than iron. The 380m long Glenfinnan viaduct is a fine example of building in concrete.

Stations

One cannot leave the work of the railway builders without a quick mention of stations. It was clear from the start that for safety reasons passengers would have to be kept apart from the trains. (At the opening of the Liverpool to Manchester railway, a government minister, William

Bridging the Tweed at Leaderfoot

Huskisson was knocked down and fatally injured.) Early stations were simple affairs of wooden huts, but soon they were being replaced with architect designed stone or brick stations. They had platforms to make it easier for the passengers to climb aboard, ticket offices, waiting rooms, toilets and often buffets providing food. They ranged from simple country stations with one platform to the glass-roofed complex at Waverley in Edinburgh and the Gothic splendour of St Enoch's in Glasgow.

The Glenfinnan viaduct

The Engine

As you can see from the illustration below, the 'Rocket' had cylinders sticking up at an angle on the outside of the boiler. Within a few years, Stephenson had improved his original design greatly. The cylinders were made horizontal which increased the stability of the engine. Once the firebox was incorporated into the boiler and the cylinders were brought inside, the engine began to be more streamlined. Other improvements followed. The boiler was lengthened to increase power and speed. The

addition of a separate bogie at the front to carry the front of the boiler made cornering easier, while trailing wheels behind the drive wheels improved stability. Samuel Hall's improved smokebox (1841) made engines less smoky and dirty.

By 1848 engines had already managed speeds of up to 67 mph, but in practice they would not normally travel at more than 40 mph. Early braking systems were jerky, which made stopping quickly dangerous when travelling at high speed. In 1870

George Westinghouse invented the automatic pressure brake and in 1875 continuous braking throughout the train was introduced. This allowed safe braking at much greater speeds. The 1889 Regulation of Railways Act made continuous braking compulsory in all trains.

Another advance which allowed faster speeds was the development of heavier steel rails and hard steel tyres for the engines. Boilers also continued to be improved in efficiency and also to be increased in size, allowing for

The Developing Steam Engine

The Rocket 1829
Stephenson's prize winning railway engine travelled at a speed of 29 mph.

The Planet 1830
Stephenson quickly improved his engines to make them more powerful and stable. This was a model on which all later engines were based.

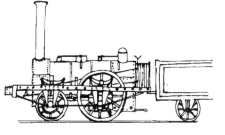

Late 19th Century/ Early 20th Century
By now steam engines were more streamlined and had longer more efficient boilers allowing for greater speeds.

1930s
The last great steam engines like the 'Mallard' averaged speeds of 70 mph and could reach over 125 mph.

The Wigtown Railway

Our new clock lichted shows the oor,
The parish church has got a toor,
And better still, up to our door,
Has come the Wigtown Railway.

Lord Galloway, gude worthy man,
The enterprise at first did plan,
An' great and sma' put to their han',
To help to make the Railway.

A while it stood at Sorbie Mill,
For want of cash to mount the hill,
But Johnston Stewart with rich guidwill,
Has brocht us up the Railway.

What gudes we noo may hae to spare,
Be't kintra growth or merchant ware,
Is sure to find a sale somewhere,
Thanks to the Wigtown Railway.

What gudes we want, be't coarse or fine,
At price accordin' to its kin'
We'll get by Scotch or English line,
And doon the Wigtown Railway.

Now fill us up nae skimpet sip,
But fill your glasses to the lip.
Three hearty cheers-Hurrah! Hip! Hip!
Hurrah! Hurrah! the Railway!

Lines composed on the arrival of the railway at Whithorn in Wigtownshire in 1875. Quoted in *A Regional History Of The Railways Of Great Britain: Volume 6* page 31 by John Thomas.

higher speeds. By 1897 the top speed reached was 90 mph and an average of 80 mph was possible on express trains. In 1904 a train topped 100 mph.

Signalling

Greater speeds were also made possible by improvements in signalling. On the first lines, the movement of trains had been directed by teams of men with flags, but as speeds increased this was clearly not safe. The big breakthrough was the telegraph. The discovery that electric signals sent along wires could move a needle across a dial marked with letters was developed by Cooke and Wheatstone. In 1837 a telegraph was installed to send signals along a railway in the south of England. This proved to be such a success that within ten years most lines were using the telegraph. When an American, Samuel Morse, developed his famous morse code, it became even easier to send signals over long distances. This made high speed rail travel much safer, with trains controlled by signals sent from one signal box to the next by telegraph.

The Carriages

There were many developments which made carriages more comfortable. On the earliest trains the first class carriages were just like road coaches put on trucks, each one separate from the next. (Some rich travellers actually had their own coaches put onto railway trucks.) Gradually though, first class travel became much more comfortable. By the 1870s sleepers and dining cars were being provided for long distance journeys. In the 1880s carriages were provided with steam heating and with communication cords for emergencies. Corridors were added to the carriages, allowing the passengers to enjoy the comfort of toilets.

Third class passengers were not so lucky. As we have seen, early third class carriages were just open trucks without even any seats. In 1844 the government passed an Act to regulate the railways. Among its provisions, it laid down that railway companies should run at least one third class train daily at a fare of a penny a mile, and that the carriages must have seats and cover from the weather. The popularity of these 'Parliamentary trains' helped the steady growth of third class travel, but conditions remained hard. Even in the 1890s third class passengers were travelling in carriages with wooden seats and no corridors.

This meant there were no toilets or eating facilities. To travel long distances third class must have required a strong bladder! Many families carried potties for the children and apparently it was also possible to purchase a device which could be worn under the clothes. To allow for the bodily needs of the passengers, trains would have occasional 15 minute stops to let them dive to the toilet and perhaps grab a cup of tea or coffee at the station buffet. Another hazard of trains without corridors was the risk of finding oneself alone in a compartment with an unpleasant character. Women on their own were particularly at risk. However, competition between the railway companies did help to improve things. The English Midland line led the way in upgrading its third class carriages so as to attract more passengers. As third class improved, second class carriages disappeared altogether on most lines.

THE IMPACT OF THE RAILWAYS

Economic Benefits—Industry

It is not surprising that the first railways appeared in industrial areas like the Monklands district in Scotland or the coalfields of Tyneside and Lancashire in England. The benefits of a good railway system were quite obvious to the coal owners and iron masters who were mainly responsible for setting up the first railway companies. The expansion of the coal mines and iron works of Central Scotland was greatly speeded up once it became possible to move heavy loads by rail.

Other industries were greatly helped by having railway transport available. For example, the Borders woollen industry flourished once the railways gave it the means to get its products to markets in central Scotland and in England. Also, since the Borders had no coal of its own, the fuel to power the mills came in by rail. Shipbuilders on the Clyde were increasingly using iron (and later steel) to build ships. The iron was carried from the furnaces of Motherwell and Coatbridge by rail. Railway transport became virtually essential for the success of any industrial concern and many companies had branch lines specially built to link them with the railway network. For example, in Clydebank there were branch lines for shipyards like Yarrows and Beardmores, and special trains were run daily to bring workers to the huge Singer factory.

Agriculture and Fisheries
Agriculture too benefited enormously. Farmers soon came to realise the value of railways for moving produce to market. Before this animals had had to be walked to the markets in the larger towns and cities. Droving cattle and sheep was a slow and costly business. It could take several weeks to get your animals to market and you risked losing some on the way. Now, thanks to the railways, cattle could be sent to market in London from Scotland in a day or so. As a result, railway junctions like Lockerbie and Newtown St Boswells developed as important centres for the buying and selling of animals. Farmers could also send fresh fruit, vegetables, milk and butter to the industrial towns every day by train. Near large towns, dairy farming and vegetable production expanded to meet the needs of town dwellers. The milk train became a daily event.

The fishing industry did well too. Previously, fish either had to be consumed locally, or preserved by salting in barrels of brine.

Now fresh fish could reach the cities every day from fishing ports like Eyemouth, Dunbar, Arbroath, Montrose and Aberdeen—to name but a few. Fresh Scottish cod, salmon or herring could be sold in Billingsgate Market in London within a day of being landed.

Communications
The railways greatly speeded up the spread of news. The newspaper industry could now use trains to send papers all over the country on the day they were published, greatly increasing their popularity and circulation. The Post Office also benefited. In 1840 Rowland Hill had invented the penny post which allowed letters to be sent all over Britain for just one penny stamp. Railways soon took over the delivery of the royal mail from coaches. Keeping in touch with distant friends and relatives was no longer a problem.

Tourism
Another new industry created by the railways was tourism. Very early on railway companies realised the potential for tourism and began to run trips to the Clyde coast and the 'Burns country'. The 'Waverley Line' through the central Borders was deliberately named for its connection with the land of Sir Walter Scott, the famous writer. Another type of railway tourism was the building of lines to golf resorts. For example a line was built down the Ayrshire coast to the Turnberry golf course which was provided with a specially built hotel.

Likewise it was the railway company which ran the Stirling to Perth line that developed the Gleneagles golfing resort and hotel. The lines to the Clyde coast resorts like Gourock and Ardrossan linked with pleasure steamer sailings to Bute and

Arran. Railway lines were built to spa towns like Moffat and Strathpeffer where wealthy people could go on health cures.

The Railway Industry
The railways themselves generated a lot of industrial development. Engines, rails, bridges, etc. needed large quantities of iron and steel, while the engine boilers demanded lots of coal to fuel them. Industries grew up to supply the needs of the railways. For instance the building of the Glasgow to Carlisle line provided a profitable business for the local brickworks which made the bricks to line tunnels and cuttings. Engineering businesses grew up to build and maintain the engines. There were several large railway engineering yards in Glasgow by the end of the 19th century. By the early 1900s Glasgow engineers were supplying engines not only to Scotland but also to France, South America and all parts of the British Empire. It is reckoned that before World War I they were turning out 800 engines a year.

Finally, it should not be forgotten that the railway companies themselves were major employers. The building of the lines obviously gave employment to thousands of workers (58,884 in Great Britain in 1850 according to an official survey), but even after they had moved on there was still work. Each station needed a station master, ticket clerks, and porters. Each train would have an engine driver, a fireman, a guard and dining car staff. Then there were engineers to look after the engines, linesmen and platesmen who maintained the lines, signalmen, level-crossing keepers, cleaners, catering staff, etc. When the station was opened in 1875 at the little town of Wick in the far north of Scotland, it had thirteen staff.

EVALUATION EXERCISE

changing technology: the railways

It is a double road constructed with flat rails, resting on blocks of durable stone. Horse power alone is used. In 1816 a locomotive engine was tried. It was intended to convey coal to Troon, but from its defective construction and ill adaptation to flat rails, it drew only ten tons at the rate of five miles an hour.

Source A is a description of the Kilmarnock to Troon Railway from *The New Statistical Account For Kilmarnock,* 1832.

Thanks to improved signalling methods and heavier track, higher speeds were becoming safer. The gradual introduction after 1875 of continuous braking throughout the train made high speed safer still. Maximum speeds which in 1884 had reached the low seventies went up between then and 1897 to an absolute maximum of 90 with 80s becoming quite common.

Source B is taken from *Railways* By G C Allan, 1960.

Source C Navvies at work on a railway cutting in the 1830s

Source D Navvies working on the approach to the Forth Bridge 1888

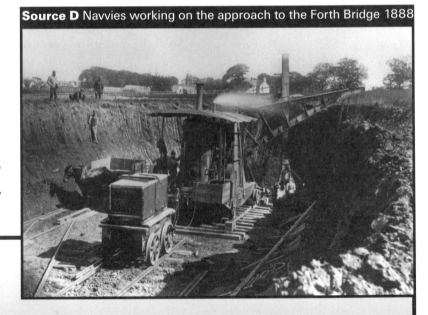

Questions

1 How valuable is Source A for finding out about early railway technology?

2 How fully does Source B describe the reasons for the increasing speeds on the railways in the later 19th century?

3 Compare Sources C and D. How useful are they for finding out about changes in the technology used by railway builders?

chapter 8

REFORM OF PARLIAMENT

What you will learn:

- that in 1830 only a few people could vote
- that by 1930 all adults were entitled to vote
- that 100 years ago women were seen as second class citizens
- that some women resorted to violent methods to get the vote

---
CONCEPTS

Democracy
Government
Social change

The Scottish Electoral System Before 1832

BURGHS		COUNTIES	
15 MPs		**30 MPs**	
1 MP For Edinburgh	14 MPs shared by 65 Burghs	27 MPs for 27 Counties	3 MPs for Bute, Caithness, Clackmannan, Cromarty, Kinross and Nairn

The Election—Total Number of voters approximately 1,000.

Four or five Burgh Councils, each one chosen from a small group of merchants. Each council chooses one Delegate.

The Delegates choose

1 Member of Parliament

The Electors—About 3,000 voters.

Owners of land over £400 value

Parchment Barons—fake voters. (They could make up nearly 50% of the voters.)

TODAY GREAT BRITAIN is a *democratic* country. This means that all citizens, whatever their wealth or position, have the right to vote for Members of Parliament and to take part in the political life of the country. Everyone over 18 years of age, with a very few exceptions, has the vote. The exceptions include criminals serving jail sentences, people who are locked up in mental hospitals, and members of the House of Lords who are already Members of Parliament. Our Parliament controls lawmaking and the raising of taxes and the gov-ernment must answer to Parliament for the way it decides to run the country. Parliament consists of two houses with the House of Lords being the less powerful. Some of the Lords are hereditary peers who inherited the right to be members, but nowadays many are life peers who have been given a seat as a reward for public service. The members of the House of Commons are elected by the voters every five years. The government is formed from the party which has the most MPs in the House of Commons.

In 1830 the British system of government was not at all democratic. Certainly Great Britain did have an elected Parliament unlike most European countries at that time. However, the *franchise* (the right to vote) was mainly limited to the rich, so only a handful of people had the vote. In some 'rotten boroughs' there were no voters at all and the local landowner appointed the MP. As voting was done in public, it was easy to put pressure on voters. Vote-fixing and corruption were normal.

THE SCOTTISH POLITICAL SYSTEM BEFORE 1832

In Scotland before 1832 there were only about 4,300 voters for a population of 2.5 million, or approximately one voter for every 600 people. The 45 Scottish seats at Westminster were shared out between the counties and the burghs.

County Elections
There were 33 Scottish counties but only 30 seats, so 6 of the

smallest counties were only represented in every second Parliament and Shetland had no MP at all. The right to vote was limited to the better-off landowners. This meant, for example, that in an area like Midlothian, with a large and prosperous population, less than 100 people had a vote. However, the greatest landowners could use their wealth to create voters. By a legal trick they could give people grants of land which existed only on paper, but which qualified them to vote. These 'parchment barons' often made up to half of the voters in Scottish county elections—and of course they voted as instructed by the landowners.

Burgh Elections

In the burghs things were no better. 66 royal burghs shared 15 seats—one MP for Edinburgh, and the other 14 representing groups of four or five burghs each. The right of a burgh to be represented in Parliament usually dated back to the Middle Ages. Burghs were run by the masters of the merchant and craft guilds, a tiny group of men who elected each other in turns onto the town council. The MPs were chosen by delegates sent by each town council. So again only a handful of people were involved and it was easy to fix elections by bribery or corruption.

A Changing Society

By the early 19th century there was much discontent with this system. Scotland and Britain were changing rapidly. New industries were growing up and many people were moving from the country to the new industrial towns to work. These new towns faced a whole range of social problems, yet they were rarely represented in Parliament. For example neither Paisley nor Greenock had an MP in spite of their size and relative importance. Middle-class industrialists

and businessmen felt frustrated that, in spite of their growing wealth, they were excluded from political power. They felt that the upper classes who controlled power did not understand the needs of business.

Working people also demanded change. They believed that the only way to get improvements in working conditions was through Parliament—but an upper-class Parliament would never listen to their demands. Middle-class industrialists and working-class activists alike felt that the old political system was a block to progress in a time of change.

THE FIRST REFORM ACT OF 1832

In 1830 the recently elected Government of the Whigs or Liberals led by Earl Grey introduced a Bill to reform Parliament. It was strongly opposed by the Tories but won widespread popular support. All over Britain there were demonstrations in favour of reform. In many towns and cities working men took to the streets to demand "the Bill, the whole Bill and nothing but the Bill". The House of Lords tried to block the Reform Bill and forced an election on the issue. However, the Whigs won this election too on a tide of popular enthusiasm. Faced with the threat of having their powers reduced, the Lords backed down. In 1832 the Bill finally became law. After all the excitement, it proved to be a very moderate reform which benefited the middle classes but did not give the vote to ordinary workers who had campaigned so hard for it.

The Terms of the Reform Act
The Act wiped out some of the worst abuses. The seats were distributed more fairly. Some were taken away from decayed and rotten burghs (old towns

Population Figures

	Scotland	UK
1831	2,364,386	24,028,584
1841	2,620,184	26,730,929
1851	2,888,742	27,390,629
1861	3,062,294	28,927,485
1871	3,360,018	31,484,661
1881	3,735,573	34,884,848
1891	4,025,647	37,732,922
1901	4,472,103	41,458,721
1911	4,760,904	42,221,615

Registered Electorate

	Scotland	UK
1830	4,300	478,000
1832	65,000	814,000
1866	105,494	1,359,163
1868	239,856	2,455,789
1883	310,441	3,152,912
1886	574,358	5,707,531

Table 8.1   Source: Various

which had long since ceased to be important) and were given instead to the new industrial towns. The rules about who qualified for the vote were tidied up. In effect the new rules gave the vote to the better-off middle-class merchants and businessmen as well as the landowners.

The Reforms in Scotland
Scotland received eight extra seats, all of which were given to the towns including some which had never been represented before. The alteration in the voting rules meant that the Scottish electorate increased from about 4,300 voters to 65,000.

The Counties
The vote was given to owners of land worth £10 per year and to tenants with long leases of land worth £10. Tenants on short leases renting land worth £50 a year were also allowed to vote. This did increase the number of voters. However, the voting was

The Six Points OF THE PEOPLE'S CHARTER.

1. A VOTE for every man twenty-one years of age, of sound mind, and not undergoing punishment for crime.

2. THE BALLOT.—To protect the elector in the exercise of his vote.

3. NO PROPERTY QUALIFICATION for Members of Parliment—thus enabling the constituencies to return the man of their choice, be he rich or poor.

4. PAYMENT OF MEMBERS, thus enabling an honest tradesman, working man, or other person, to serve a constituency, when taken from his business to attend to the interests of the country.

5. EQUAL CONSTITUENCIES, securing the same amount of representation for the same number of electors, instead of allowing small constituencies to swamp the votes of large ones.

6. ANNUAL PARLIAMENTS, thus presenting the most effectual check to bribery and intimidation, since though a constituency might be bought once in seven years (even with the ballot), no purse could buy a constituency (under a system of universal suffrage) in each ensuing twelvemonth; and since members, when elected for a year only, would not be able to defy and betray their constituents as now.

still done publicly, so in practice the great landowners remained in control. A tenant farmer who voted against the wishes of his landlord risked not having his lease renewed.

The Burghs

Edinburgh and Glasgow each got two MPs while Aberdeen, Dundee and Perth got one each, as did the new towns of Greenock and Paisley. Other industrial towns like Kilmarnock got a share of an MP. The vote was given to all householders of property worth £10 per year (ie. the better off). This greatly increased the number of voters and made the burgh elections much more open to the pressure of public opinion.

THE CHARTISTS

The Whigs were well satisfied with their work. They believed that their reform was a good and lasting solution to the question of how the British government should be run. The idea of giving the vote to ordinary working men would have shocked them. Poor people had little or no property and therefore no stake in society, so why should they be given any say in such matters as taxation and lawmaking?

However, for the Radicals the 1832 Reform Act had not gone nearly far enough. The Radicals believed that British society must be completely reformed to make it fairer. They thought that the first step to getting any improvement in conditions was to win the right to vote and to get working men into Parliament. Many poor people endured low wages and dreadful conditions of work in the factories and mines. They lived in overcrowded and insanitary slums in the new factory towns. There was much unrest among the working classes. Out of this popular discontent grew the Chartist movement which was founded in 1838. The Chartists aimed to win the vote by taking their demands to Parliament in the form of a giant petition—the People's Charter. In the Charter they put forward six basic demands:

1. The vote for all men over 21.
2. Payment for Members of Parliament.
3. No property qualification for MPs.
4. Equal sized constituencies.
5. Annual elections for Parliament.
6. A secret ballot.

These ideas may seem very moderate to us now, but to the ruling classes of the time they seemed dangerous and revolutionary. On three occasions, in 1839, 1842 and 1848, petitions signed by hundreds of thousands of ordinary people were presented to Parliament. Each time Parliament rejected the People's Charter. The last petition in 1848 was treated with ridicule after it was shown that some of the 2 million signatures were in fact foolish forgeries. (Queen Victoria, for example!)

The Chartist movement failed largely because it was torn apart by in-fighting. It split between the moderates led by William Lovett and Francis Place who wanted to campaign peacefully for the vote and a more extreme group led by Fergus O'Connor who talked of using violence. In Scotland it was an east/west split. In Edinburgh the Chartists—mainly skilled craftsmen—favoured the idea of "moral suasion" and protests took the form of peaceful marches. Glasgow, with its large population of poor factory workers was much more extreme. The Glasgow Chartists supported the use of physical force and the worst violence of the period—the Bread Riots of 1848—took place in Glasgow. Another reason for the failure of the Chartist movement was that it had little support outside the working classes, so it was short of more influential and better educated people who could organise it effectively.

The Chartist movement reached its greatest strength in the 1840s because this was a time of economic recession—the 'Hungry Forties'—which brought great suffering to the poor. As the economy picked up in the 1850s Chartism died. It had had too many leaders with too many different ideas. For the next 50 years, working-class men put their energy into the Trade Union movement instead. It seemed to promise more immediate practical gains than the dreams of the Chartists.

THE SECOND REFORM ACT 1867

As we have seen, the reformers of 1832 thought that their Reform Act was a once and for all measure. However, by the 1860s the public mood was once again in favour of a Parliamentary reform which would match the changes taking place in British society.

It was the Whigs or Liberals who first proposed a new reform in 1866, but they were defeated in Parliament and forced to resign. The resulting election gave power to the Tories. However, the mood of the country was now so much in favour of reform that they were forced to bring in their own Reform Bill. As their leader, Lord Derby, cynically remarked, they would "dish the

Whigs" by stealing their policies. The Tories intended their Bill to be a very moderate affair, but as it went through Parliament the Whigs managed to amend it in various ways. By the time the Reform Act was passed it was actually more extreme than the one originally proposed by the Whigs in 1866!

The Terms of the Second Reform Act
Once again the seats in Parliament were redistributed to take account of the continuing changes in population distribution at this time. The right to vote was extended—particularly in the towns where the granting of the vote to male adult householders meant that, for the first time, some working-class men could vote.

The Reforms in Scotland
The Scottish version of the Act which was passed in 1868 increased the Scottish electorate to 230,000 voters. It gave the vote in the burghs to all male adult householders and, in addition, to lodgers paying £10 or more per year rent. This gave the vote to some of the better-off working classes—craftsmen and skilled workers. However this only applied to those living in the burghs. In the counties, owners of land worth £5 per year and tenants paying over £14 per year rent got the vote—in effect the owners and tenants of larger farms. The vote did not extend to the crofters and farm labourers who were the bulk of the rural population, nor did it go to the craftsmen and skilled workers in small country towns.

The other weakness of the Act was that it had done nothing about the voting methods. The lack of a secret ballot meant that employers and landlords could still put pressure on voters, especially in the county seats. Quite

simply, the tenant farmer who was rash enough to vote against the wishes of his landlord would not have his lease renewed.

POLITICAL PARTIES IN THE 19TH CENTURY

In the 19th century the two main parties were the Tories or Conservatives and the Whigs or Liberals. By the middle of the 19th century both of these parties were changing.

The Tories in the early 19th century had been very reactionary—opposed to any reforms. However after the First Reform Act a new group of younger, more go-ahead men took over the Party. The change is reflected in the new name of the Party—Conservative—which arose from the promise made by the new leader, Robert Peel, that the Tories would not try to undo the 1832 Reform Act, but would conserve it.

Benjamin Disraeli, who led the Conservatives in the 1860s and '70s, guided the Party further along the path of reform. As a member of Lord Derby's Cabinet, Disraeli was largely responsible for the 1867 Reform Act, and as Prime Minister between 1874 and 1880 he carried out many important social reforms. Disraeli taught his Party that if it was to win the support of the new working-class voters then aristocratic influence must be combined with a fatherly concern for the lower classes. His reforms were always of a practical type—improvements in working-class housing and public health measures, for example. Disraeli also developed the policy of Imperialism—building up the British Empire overseas.

The Whig Party too was changing. During the 1840s and '50s the Whigs picked up new supporters from various directions. Some of them were Radicals—politicians who wanted the vote for all classes. They saw the Whigs as the party most sympathetic to the lower classes. Others were former Tories who had supported Peel's reforming views.

Like the Tories, the Whigs became known by a new name—Liberals. The greatest Liberal Prime Minister of the century was a former Tory, William Gladstone, who was Disraeli's great rival. He was responsible for many important reforms. His reforms were often of less obvious practical value than Disraeli's since his concern was to remove the basic inequalities and allow all citizens the same chances in life. So, for instance, he removed religious barriers to university education and opened up the civil service and the army to promotion by ability rather than by social class. It is really not surprising that the major reforms in the voting system in the later 19th century were his work.

In the 1880s the Liberal Party split over Gladstone's plan to end unrest in Ireland by giving it a separate Parliament. Some Liberals broke away and joined the Conservatives. The Conservatives opposed the idea of Home Rule for Ireland, seeing it as a threat to the unity of Great Britain—hence their other name, Unionists.

GLADSTONE'S POLITICAL REFORMS

The Ballot Act 1872
During his first spell as Prime Minister, the great Liberal leader Gladstone was responsible for for one of the most important reforms of all in the voting system—the Ballot Act. Until this time, voters had had to cast their vote publicly which made it easy for powerful men such as landlords and employers to intimidate them.

The Ballot Act meant that voting was now done in secrecy which allowed working people to vote as they really wanted.

The Corrupt Practices Act 1883
This act took the principle of fair voting further by outlawing bribery of the voters in any way. Before this it was not unusual for rich candidates to offer the voters free whisky or dinners in return for their support.

The Third Reform Act 1884–85
Gladstone was also responsible for bringing in a third Reform Bill which planned to extend the right to vote to many more working men and also to remove the differences in voting rights between the burghs and the counties. His proposals won widespread support in Scotland. Conservative attempts to block the Bill led to a mass meeting on Glasgow Green, with protesters carrying portraits of their hero, Gladstone among their banners.

The Third Reform Act of 1884 (1885 in Scotland) extended the vote to all male adult householders, thus removing the inequality between the burghs and the counties which had existed since 1867. In Scotland this meant that over 560,500 men, or 60% of all adult males, now had the vote, and many working-class men could now qualify as voters. However, poor unskilled workers, many of them Irish immigrants, were still unlikely to be voters.

The Act also brought a further redistribution of the seats. Small towns lost their right to a separate seat while larger towns and cities had seats allocated according to their population. In effect Britain was moving towards the present system of constituencies of roughly equal size. The number of Scottish seats was increased to 72.

A NEW PARTY—THE RISE OF LABOUR

For most of the 19th century the Liberals were seen as the party most sympathetic to the working-class. Radicals campaigning for working-class issues usually stood as Liberals in elections. However, the Liberal Party was dominated by middle and upper class politicians, and the Radicals had only limited influence. One result of the extension of the franchise was that some working-class politicians began to think about forming a genuine working-class party. This was not going to be easy because MPs were not paid, so it was almost impossible for someone who did not already have money to be an MP.

In 1888 the Scottish Labour Party was founded by James Keir Hardie, a miner and militant trade unionist. His attempts to be elected as an MP for a Scottish seat failed, but in 1892 he was elected as MP for a London constituency. Keir Hardie was the first true Labour MP. Much to the horror of the other members, he arrived at the House of Commons wearing a cloth cap instead of the usual top hat! In 1893 he was involved in the founding of the Independent Labour Party of Great Britain and in 1900 the Labour Representation Committee was set up to work for the election of Labour MPs to Parliament. Its secretary was another Scot, J Ramsay MacDonald who, in 1924, was to become the first ever Labour Prime Minister. In the General Election of 1906 the new Labour Party won 29 seats, including 2 in Scotland.

Another 24 were Lib/Labs—Radicals backed by the Liberal Party but sympathetic to the aims of Labour. The new party got its financial backing mainly from the Trade Union movement. Every union raised a subscription from its members to help support strikes, sick workers, etc. Now it was agreed by the Trades Union Congress that each union would contribute money from its funds to pay for MPs who would promote Labour policies in Parliament.

The Party's ideas came largely from the Socialist movement which grew out of the industrial revolution. Thinkers, who were appalled by the poverty and hardship endured by industrial workers, put forward the idea of abolishing private ownership. They argued that factories and businesses should be owned by the people who worked in them, so that those who worked to produce the wealth would get a fair share of the profits. Extreme socialists followed the ideas and teachings of Karl Marx who said that change could come about only as a result of a working class revolution in which the ruling classes would be wiped out. However, such violent ideas won little support from members of the Labour Party.

THE LIBERALS AND REFORM 1906–14

In 1906 the Liberals came to power again after ten years in opposition. They were committed to a programme of social reforms, but the extra taxation which was needed to pay for them brought the Government into direct conflict with the House of Lords. The Chancellor, David Lloyd George, in his 'People's Budget' of 1909, proposed several taxes which would hit the rich, including a tax on land values. The House of Lords was dominated by the Conservative Party, whose members were the wealthy landowners on whom the new taxes would fall most heavily. They threw out the budget and provoked a major constitutional crisis. This was by no means the first time that Liberal policies had been frustrated by the blocking power of the Lords, but never before had the Upper House blocked the budget.

The Liberal Government decided that enough was enough—the Lords must have their wings clipped. They fought and won two general elections on the issue and finally in 1911 brought in the Parliament Act which greatly reduced the power of the Lords. The Lords were forced to accept the Act by the threat that if they did not, the King would create so many new Liberal peers that the Conservatives in the House would be swamped. The Parliament Act laid down that in future the Lords could only delay bills passed by the Commons for a maximum of two years. Moreover, they could not touch the budget or any other finance bills at all. Also, the length of parliaments was

The Main Political Reforms 1830–1914

Date	Reform	Effects
1832	First Reform Act	Reorganised seats more fairly and cut out the worst abuses in voting. Gave the vote to upper middle classes.
1867	Second Reform Act	Extended the right to vote in burghs to adult male householders. Gave the vote to most of the middle class and some workers in towns.
1872	Ballot Act	Voting by secret ballot introduced. Landlords and bosses could now no longer influence votes of their tenants or workers.
1883	Corrupt Practices Act	Limited spending by candidates at elections & stopped bribery of voters.
1884	Third Reform Act	Extended the vote in the counties to male adult householders. Many better-off workers now had the right to vote.
1911	Parliament Act	Limited the power of the House of Lords. General elections were to be held every five years.
1911	Payment of MPs	Allowed working-class men a better chance of standing for Parliament.

reduced from seven to five years. The Liberals also passed an Act for MPs to be paid a salary of £400 a year. This was a great boon to the Labour Party. They did Labour another favour too. In 1910 a man called Osbourne had successfully taken his union to court to stop it from using union funds to support the Labour Party. The Liberals amended the law to allow trade unions to have a separate political fund in future.

These reforms marked another important stage in the march to democracy. However, in one area the Liberal government was stubbornly opposed to reform—the issue of votes for women.

THE STATUS OF WOMEN IN THE 19TH CENTURY

Women and the Vote

You may have noticed that so far we have talked only of votes for men. In the 19th century, women were very much second class citizens who were under the control of their menfolk and had few rights. They were seen as weak and foolish creatures. The Bible was quoted to support the view that women were lesser beings who had to be kept in their place in case they led men astray with their devilish feminine wiles. Before the 19th century there was little future for women outside marriage. Unmarried women stayed at home or went into service, living in the homes of their masters. Any woman rash enough to try living on her own was likely to be branded as a prostitute.

With the coming of the factory age, women (along with children) were seen as a good source of cheap labour. Women factory workers did the low-paid unskilled jobs. The trade unions, dominated by men, rarely took much interest in their rights. By the end of the 19th century, laws had been passed to improve working conditions in large factories and mines. However, many women worked in the 'sweated industries' in small workshops which were not covered by the law. For example, the women who worked sewing clothes usually had to work very long hours in cramped ill-lit cellars and attics, for perhaps as little as a penny an hour.

For better-off women too, life was very restricted. They had little chance of a proper education or a career of their own. The only acceptable jobs for a lady from a good home were either a governess to a rich family's children or else a companion to a wealthy widow. Such work, though, was considered to be a dreadful come-down—only for those unlucky women who had failed to get married and had no-one to support them. Middle-class women were not expected to work but had to devote their lives to being wives and mothers. Their chief duty was to be obedient and ornamental, to set off the manliness and authority of their husbands. Since they had servants to do any hard work, they had little to occupy them.

Nevertheless, a middle-class man would be insulted by the suggestion that his wife might take a job to fill her time—as if he could not support her himself! While working-class women struggled working long hours for little pay, for middle-class women the chief problem all too often was boredom. It was from the leisured middle classes that the demand for votes for women first came.

The fight to get the vote was seen as part of a larger fight to improve women's rights. In the middle of the 19th century, a woman was seen as her husband's property. She had no right to refuse his sexual demands and for many women marriage meant a continual string of pregnancies (since no contraception was available), with the ill health that caused. Any money or property she took into the marriage became his. If she left her husband she would become penniless—even if he was a brutal drunkard or an adulterer, he kept all the property. (Small wonder that divorces were rare.) The children were his property too, and if he died it was his male relations who got custody of them, not his wife.

WOMEN'S RIGHTS

The First Suffragists
At the time of the Second Re-

	Making Progress
1857	A woman abandoned by her husband could keep her own earnings.
1870	Women were allowed to vote for the new school boards.
1880	Women could vote in county council elections. (They had been able to vote for town councils since 1834.)
1880	Married women were given control of their own property. It no longer automatically became their husband's when they married.
1886	If a man abandoned his wife he had to pay her maintenance. If he died she became legal guardian of their children.
1889	The Universities Act required universities to admit women.
1891	A man could no longer lock his wife up.
1894	Women could stand for election to local councils.

Pro-suffragette demonstration, Edinburgh, 1900

form Act of 1867 women began to campaign for suffrage—the right to vote. The first Suffrage Societies were set up in that year in London, Manchester and Edinburgh. The Edinburgh society was led by Priscilla McLaren, wife of a Radical MP. It was mainly wealthy ladies who had the time to be involved in the campaign, not working-class women. They held meetings, drew up petitions and wrote books and pamphlets to draw attention to their cause.

In the next ten years 2 million signatures were collected in Scotland in support of the vote for women. Since few male politicians were prepared to take them seriously, nothing was changed. The 1884 Reform Act was a great disappointment to the women.

Education
However, progress was made in other areas. Women's opportunities were expanded when education became available to every child after 1870. Not only were girls now educated as well as boys, but the expansion of education brought a great many new jobs for women as teachers. (For a long time though, they were paid less than men.) Other new jobs were opening up to women, for example in offices where they could work as typists. Nursing too had become a respectable occupation for young women, due to the work of Florence Nightingale.

In higher education great advances were made, thanks largely to the determination of women like Elizabeth Garrett Anderson and Sophia Jex-Blake. They studied medicine at St Andrews and Edinburgh, but the universities would not allow women to sit the final exams even though they had completed the classes. They had to go abroad to qualify as doctors. Thanks to the struggle of these women to gain recognition, many universities and colleges began to let women onto their courses. Women were beginning to break into other male dominated professions like the law. No longer could men argue that women were too stupid to be allowed to vote.

Elizabeth Garrett Anderson went on to run a clinic in London which specialised in treating women. One of her admirers was Dr Elsie Inglis who set up a hospital for women in Edinburgh. For the first time some women could get sympathetic medical treatment from doctors of their own sex.

Women's Working Conditions
Among working-class women too, things were changing. The women workers of the Bryant and May match factory went on strike. They had plenty to complain of—miserable pay, long hours, and dangerous working conditions. They were helped in their campaign by a leading suffragist, Annie Besant. Their success encouraged other women to start trying to improve their

working conditions. Women also began to get much more involved in trade unions.

Some Progress

The improving status of women led to several changes in the law. However, there was still no progress towards getting women the vote for Parliament. After forty years of peaceful campaigning, some women began to feel that stronger action was needed.

THE SUFFRAGETTES

The WSPU

In 1903 a new organisation was set up. It was called the Women's Social and Political Union and its founders were Mrs Emmeline Pankhurst, the widow of a Labour politician, and her daughters Christabel and Sylvia. Mrs Pankhurst's slogan was 'Deeds not Words', and she and her followers soon made their presence felt. They held demonstrations, interrupted political meetings, and chained themselves to public buildings such as the Houses of Parliament, so that the police could not easily stop them from shouting their slogans. Soon they had won a nickname—the Suffragettes—first used by a newspaper to describe these noisy campaigners for the suffrage.

The Suffragettes had great hopes that the reforming Liberal Government which came into power in 1906 might do something for them. They were soon disappointed. The Liberal leaders showed no interest whatsoever in votes for women. In 1911 the Suffragette campaign became more militant. They were quite prepared to break the law as long as it got them into the newspapers. Shop windows were smashed, golf courses were vandalised, paintings were slashed, burning rags were stuffed into

letter boxes and telephone wires were cut.

Hunger Strikes

When women were sent to jail for these offences, they continued their protest by going on hunger strike. At first the government ordered the women to be force-fed. This was a dreadful, painful business with the risk of serious injury to the prisoner. The Suffragettes were able to make great propaganda from this, accusing the government of torture. The government was in a cleft stick. It was condemned for brutality to women, but it would look just as bad if women were allowed to die of starvation. Its answer was the Prisoners' Temporary Discharge Act of 1913. Women on hunger strike were let out of prison when their health started to suffer. After a week or two they would be brought back to continue their sentence. This was nicknamed the Cat and Mouse Act by the Suffragettes.

Growing Violence

In the years before the First World War, the women's campaign became more and more violent. There were firebomb attacks on the houses of important men and on public buildings. The women hoped that the financial cost of these attacks might make men think again. In 1913 Emily Wilding Davison was killed when she ran out in front of the King's horse at the Derby. To the Suffragettes she was a martyr to the cause, but to many men such behaviour was foolish and irresponsible. It seemed to prove that women were too silly to be trusted with the vote. The activities of the Suffragettes embarrassed the government, but they still showed no sign of giving in to the women's demands. Indeed, it has to be said that many women disapproved of the WSPU's tactics.

The Women's Freedom League was set up in 1907 by Mrs Despard and other women who disliked the methods used by Mrs Pankhurst and the WSPU. It later joined up with other groups in the National Union of Women's Suffrage Societies (NUWSS). These groups all rejected violence and continued to campaign peacefully for the vote.

SCOTTISH SUFFRAGETTES

The Scottish WSPU

By 1906 there was a Scottish branch of the WSPU with its headquarters in Glasgow. It got a lot of support from women artists and actresses in the city such as Jessie Newberry, and Margaret and Annie Fraser. The most prominent Scottish Suffragette was Flora Drummond, a typist from Arran. She became one of Mrs Pankhurst's closest followers. Although she was only slightly over five feet tall, she had a tremendous personality and great organising talent. As General Officer of the WSPU she was the organiser of the big marches and demonstrations in London. The tiny 'General' became a well-known figure riding at the head of the processions on horseback. She was arrested several times. In 1908, the Scottish Suffragettes campaigned vigorously against the Liberals in four Scottish by-elections. One particular target was Winston Churchill who was standing for the safe Liberal seat of Dundee and who was a well-known opponent of the Suffragettes. He did not lose the election, but the Liberal majority was cut by a considerable amount.

Militancy

As in England the Scottish movement had become more militant by 1913. There were acid attacks on letter boxes and shop windows were smashed in Glasgow. The railway line between Glasgow and Carlisle was blown up. The King's portrait in the National Gallery was slashed. Many buildings were attacked with firebombs, including the racecourse buildings at Ayr and Kelso, the Royal Observatory in Edinburgh, the Gatty Marine Laboratory at St Andrews, and also several railway stations and private mansions. The Prime Minister, Herbert Asquith, was ambushed by two Suffragettes on Lossiemouth golf course. A royal visit to Scotland in 1914 led to several demonstrations. Mrs Pankhurst and other leading Suffragettes from England made regular tours in Scotland to speak to their supporters. When Mrs Pankhurst visited Glasgow in 1914, she was due to be rearrested under the Cat and Mouse Act. She was smuggled into the hall in a laundry basket and onto a platform defended with barbed wire and women carrying Indian clubs. When the police moved in to arrest her a riot broke out.

Non-militant Action

Many Scottish women rejected the violence of the WSPU and joined the NUWSS. The NUWSS worked by using rational arguments to highlight the unfair treatment of women. For example, they set up an exhibition in Glasgow about the plight of women in the sweated trades; and they publicised the case of the Dundee sheriff who gave one man 40 days in prison for stealing a bag of sugar, while another was given just 14 days for sexually assaulting a young girl. Their peaceful campaigning won much support for the women's cause including the backing of thirty five Scottish town councils and many church ministers. However, their petitions had no more effect on Prime Minister Herbert Asquith than the violence of the extremists. In 1914 he refused to meet their delegation.

Women and the War

It looked as if the Suffragettes and the Liberal government were total enemies. Nonetheless, when the war with Germany broke out in August 1914, the women immediately called a truce and most women declared their support for the government. Suffragette leaders like Mrs Pankhurst and Flora Drummond now diverted their energy into recruiting women for war work. They hoped that the war would give them a chance to show what women could really do.

Women played a vital part in the war effort. In the factories they took over men's jobs, freeing them for fighting. Thousands of women worked in the munitions factories, often in dangerous conditions, making the guns and bullets needed by the soldiers. Women joined the Land Army to help grow the nation's food. They drove buses and trains, worked as police officers and as posties. They joined the Army, Navy and Air Force to work as drivers, nurses and office staff. At the start of the war, Dr Elsie Inglis offered to organise a field hospital. At first her offer was ignored by the government, but she went on with her work and set up the

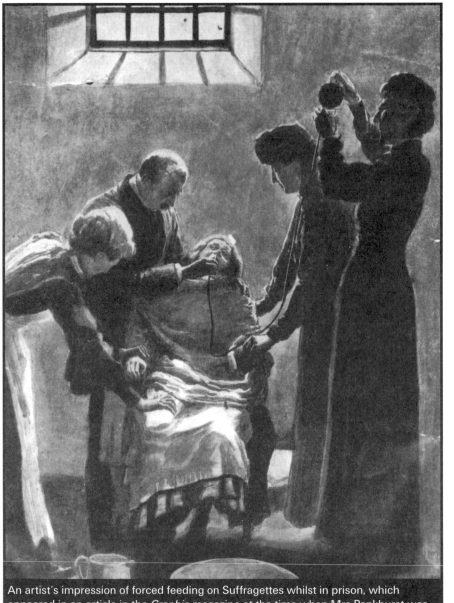

An artist's impression of forced feeding on Suffragettes whilst in prison, which appeared in an article in the *Graphic* magazine at the time when Mrs Pankhurst was imprisoned.

Scottish Women's Hospitals. By 1915 they were doing vital work in France and Serbia, often in dangerous circumstances close to the front line fighting. The work of Dr Inglis and the many other women like her greatly impressed the men and brought about a complete change in attitudes. By 1916 even Mr Asquith was agreeing that women could no longer be denied the vote in view of their huge contribution to the war effort.

THE VOTE –AT LAST!

In 1918 women got their reward. The Representation of the People Act, which gave the vote to all men over 21, also gave women the vote for the first time. However, women were still not given equality with men. Only women over 30 got the vote and they had to be householders, the wives of householders, or university graduates. Men still believed that women were more impulsive and emotional than men, so only mature women could be trusted to vote sensibly! It took another ten years of campaigning until, in 1928, a Conservative government changed the law to give all women over 21 the vote. So much had male attitudes altered by then that there was hardly any real opposition.

Were the Suffragettes right to use violence? Certainly they antagonised many men by their actions. The government in 1914 would not give women the vote as that would have seemed like giving in to force. In 1918 they made it very clear that the vote was a reward for the women's war work, not the result of the Suffragette campaign. It has been claimed that it was the non-militant groups which really won the respect of men and that the Suffragettes just got women a bad name. The question is whether, if all women had stuck

Anna Munro, national organiser of Women's Freedom League from 1908 to 1912

to peaceful methods, they would have got the same amount of attention from politicians and newspapers.

Votes for All

As we have seen, all men over 21 were given the vote by the Representation of the People Act of 1918. Like the women, British working men were rewarded for the sacrifices they had made in the war. The last property restrictions on voting rights were removed and once all women got the vote in 1928, Britain

could at last be described as a democratic country. There have been two other changes since then. In the 1949 Parliament Act, the power of the Lords was further reduced: they can now only hold up bills for one year. In 1969 another Representation of the People Act gave the vote to everyone over 18 years of age. It is interesting to look back to the demands of the Chartists and work out how far these 'revolutionary' demands have now been accepted as normal.

EVALUATION EXERCISE

parliamentary reform

The following activities refer to information contained in the chapter and in Sources A–E.

Sources A – C are all concerned with the fight to extend voting rights to working-class voters during the 19th century. **Sources D and E** are connected with the militant Suffragette campaign of the years before 1914.

Source A is from a speech in the House of Commons by Robert Lowe in March 1866.

> If the (Reform) Bill is passed it is certain that we shall see the working classes in the majority in the constituencies. Look what this implies. If you want ignorance, if you want drunkenness, or if you want impulsive, unre-flecting and violent people, where do you look for them? Do you go to the top or to the bottom?

Source B is from a speech in the House of Commons by William Gladstone in April 1866.

> *Since 1832 every kind of beneficial change has been in operation in favour of the working classes. Religious influences are more active. The civilising powers of education have been brought into existence for the mass of the people. Newspapers are circulated by the million carrying home to all classes accounts of public affairs. Can anything be more unwise than to refuse to recognise the increasing fitness of the working classes for the exercise of political power?*

Source D This is from the *Memories of Helen Crawfurd*, a Scottish member of the WSPU. It was probably written during the 1940s.

In March 1912 the women Suffragettes had adopted more drastic methods. Houses had been burned down and windows broken … .
The heroism of many of the women militants in their hunger strikes called forth admiration, and an increase in membership of the Suffrage Societies. The respectable non-militant societies had neither the dramatic nor spectacular appeal of the Women's Social and Political Union. Mrs Pankhurst's arrests and her hunger strikes made many new recruits.

THE RESULT of the Mid Lanark election showed the pressing need there was for an organisation in Scotland which would let the workers exercise their voting powers to their own advantage. Since April Mr Keir Hardie has been diverting most of his spare time to the work of organising a distinct Labour Party, and on Saturday 25th August a conference was held in Glasgow to formally give birth to the new movement.

Source C is from an article in *The Democrat* newspaper in September 1888 by J Keir Hardie.

If, instead of Mrs Pankhurst and her friends making such scenes, they were to follow the methods of the Women's Suffrage League, the vote would be won. All honour to these ladies and success to them, and let the WSPU take a leaf from their book.

Source E is from a letter in *The Glasgow Herald* July 1913.

Questions

1 Read Sources A and B and compare the attitudes of the two speakers to the question of votes for the working classes.

2 How valuable are these sources for telling us about the background to the passing of the Second Reform Bill in 1867?

3 How reliable is Source C as evidence for the origins of the Labour Party?

4 How valuable is Source D for telling us about the militant Suffragette movement?

5 Compare the attitude of the writers of Sources D and E to the question of militancy.

6 How reliable is the picture on page 88 for telling us about the treatment of Suffragette hunger strikers?

INDEX